ADVENT/CHRISTMAS

proclamation 6

Interpreting the Lessons of the Church Year

E. Elizabeth Johnson

ADVENT/CHRISTMAS

PROCLAMATION 6 | SERIES C

FORTRESS PRESS | MINNEAPOLIS

PROCLAMATION 6
Interpreting the Lessons of the Church Year
Series C, Advent/Christmas

Copyright © 1997 Augsburg Fortress. All rights reserved. Except for brief quotations in critical articles or reviews, no part of this book may be reproduced in any manner without prior written permission of the publisher. Write to: Augsburg Fortress, 426 S. Fifth St., Box 1209, Minneapolis, MN 55440.

Scripture quotations, unless otherwise indicated, are from the New Revised Standard Version Bible, copyright © 1989 by the Division of Christian Education of the National Council of Churches in the U.S.A. and are used by permission.

Cover design: Ellen Maly
Text design: David Lott

The Library of Congress has cataloged the first four volumes of Series A as follows:

Proclamation 6, Series A: interpreting the lessons of the church
  year.
    p.   cm.
    Contents: [1] Advent/Christmas / J. Christiaan Beker — [2] Epiphany / Susan K. Hedahl — [3] Lent / Peter J. Gomes — [4] Holy Week / Robin Scroggs.
    ISBN 0-8006-4207-4 (v. 1 : alk. paper) — ISBN 0-8006-4208-2 (v. 2 : alk. paper) — ISBN 0-8006-4209-0 (v. 3 : alk. paper) — ISBN 0-8006-4210-4 (v. 4 : alk. paper).
    1. Bible—Homiletical use. 2. Bible—liturgical lessons, English.
BS534.5P74 1995
251—dc20   95-4622
                                                                              CIP

   Series C:
   Advent/Christmas / E. Elizabeth Johnson—ISBN 0-8006-4231-7
   Epiphany / Richard I. Pervo—ISBN 0-8006-4232-5
   Lent / Bernhard W. Anderson —ISBN 0-8006-4233-3
   Holy Week / Patricia Wilson-Kastner—ISBN 0-8006-4234-1
   Easter / L. William Countryman—ISBN 0-8006-4235-X
   Pentecost 1 / Terence E. Fretheim—ISBN 0-8006-4236-8
   Pentecost 2 / James L. Boyce—ISBN 0-8006-4237-6
   Pentecost 3 / William L. Holladay—ISBN 0-8006-4238-4

The paper used in this publication meets the minimum requirements of American National Standard for Information Sciences—Permanence of Paper for Printed Library Materials, ANSI Z329.48-1948.

Manufactured in the U. S. A.   AF 1-4231

01   00   99   98   97   1   2   3   4   5   6   7   8   9   10

Contents

First Sunday in Advent	7
Second Sunday in Advent	19
Third Sunday in Advent	27
Fourth Sunday in Advent	34
The Nativity of Our Lord 1 *Christmas Eve*	39
The Nativity of Our Lord 2 *Christmas Day*	46
First Sunday after Christmas	52
The Name of Jesus (January 1)	62
Second Sunday after Christmas	72

First Sunday in Advent

Lectionary	First Lesson	Psalm	Second Lesson	Gospel
Revised Common	Jer. 33:14-16	Ps. 25:1-10	I Thess. 3:9-13	Luke 21:25-36
Episcopal (BCP)	Zech. 14:4-9	Psalm 50 or 50:1-6	I Thess. 3:9-13	Luke 21:25-31
Roman Catholic	Jer. 33:14-16	Ps. 25:1, 4-5, 8-9, 10, 14	I Thess. 3:12—4:2	Luke 21:25-28, 34-36
Lutheran (LBW)	Jer. 33:14-16	Ps. 25:1-9	I Thess. 3:9-13	Luke 21:25-36 or Luke 19:28-40

FIRST LESSON: JEREMIAH 33:14-16; ZECHARIAH 14:4-9

Jeremiah 33:14-16. One consequence of the church year's beginning a month before the secular calendar changes is that we remind ourselves again that our understanding of time and our experience of it are different from those of the culture around us. As we prepare year after year for Jesus' birth we claim new and renewed meaning for the present from our history. But when we announce the promise of Jesus' return in glory we also acknowledge that the present reality—for all its grace, mercy, and peace—still does not encompass everything that we rightly expect from God. Advent is the season when the church is most self-conscious about the "not yet" of its redemption, even as it rejoices in the "already" of the incarnation and God's present engagement with the world. As cultural celebrations of—or worse, manipulations of—Christmas intrude earlier and earlier into the fall, it is easy for the church's own internal clock to be knocked out of synch, and the church is easily seduced away from its task of waiting at this time of year by the culture's wallowing in sentimentalism and its glorification of material abundance. Advent thus functions both to orient—to set us about the work of preparation and anticipation, and to disorient—to set us at odds with conventional ways of marking time and valuing human experience and to stir up in us awareness of the unfinished character of redemption.

The First Sunday's text from Jeremiah is an apt beginning for the church's reflection on its experience of time out of time. Although the literary context sets the oracle in the preexilic period of Jeremiah's career when he is still "confined in the court of the guard" (33:1), it is in fact a postexilic piece that a later editor has inserted after the fact, probably during the Persian period, perhaps somewhere between 450 and 400 B.C.E. The passage thus embodies the disjuncture between what is and what ought to be in the life of the people of God.

The later prophet quotes Jeremiah's own words from 23:5-6, a promise from God that a real king will eventually replace the weak puppet Zedekiah (note the wordplay on Zedekiah's name in 23:6), and gently recasts the prophecy from a later perspective. The name "the LORD is our righteousness" (or "vindication") is in this latter passage not given to the Branch, the Davidic monarch who will attend to the people as his predecessors have not (cf. 23:2), but rather to Judah and Jerusalem (33:16). There yet remains in this later prophecy the promise of a royal Branch, but the reprise in 33:17-18 of Nathan's oracle to David from 2 Samuel 7 ("David shall never lack a man to sit on the throne . . .") postpones the fulfillment of that prophecy to allow for the current experience of the postexilic community. The immediate future of God's faithfulness is not yet seen in a human monarch, but is already visible to a degree in the royal city itself and its righteous inhabitants who worship God in the restored Temple. In the terms of the new promise, God's vindication is manifest in the reinhabited and restored city even as the prophet affirms the ultimate reestablishment of the monarchy.

It might be possible to read this passage, somewhat cynically, as a result of the failure of prophecy. Jeremiah's postexilic interpreter might appear to take the sting out of disappointed hopes by altering the original promise to say, "Do not worry that Jeremiah's prediction of a Branch has not been confirmed; it was never meant to be a particular monarch who would execute justice in the land." The following verses, however (17-22), are among the most impassioned assertions of the permanency of God's covenant with David to be found in Scripture. This means that Jeremiah's interpreter does not *replace* hope in a Davidic monarch with hope in the renewed city's faithfulness, but rather *interprets* the original hope by making room in it for his own time as a period of God's active involvement without relinquishing confidence in God's future restoration of the dynasty. The Persians allow the people to live and worship in the city, and Jeremiah's interpreter says this is God's doing as much as will be the eventual fulfillment of Jeremiah's prophecy of the Branch. The difference between a recasting of prophecy after it has apparently failed and this kind of interpretation of prophecy is a function of motivation as much as content. The latter is motivated not by fear of the prophet's being proved wrong but by the conviction that God remains faithful *in* our experience rather than *despite* it.

The church's time of waiting for redemption too is marked by God's engagement with the world even as the fullness of restoration remains to be seen. The Christian preacher who takes up the text of Jer. 33:14-16 is therefore in somewhat the same existential situation as its anonymous author:

FIRST SUNDAY IN ADVENT

both look to the tradition to announce God's promise of redemption in a world that is clearly not yet redeemed. The preacher is called with Jeremiah's descendant to affirm the trustworthiness of a promise that has not yet been kept even as he or she looks in the present for signs of its ultimate fulfillment. The triumph of God's glory is still beyond our reach, and the creation yet groans as it awaits its redemption (cf. Rom. 8:22), but even now the gathered people of God can have confidence in God's future because the love of God transforms the present. Our reappropriation of the prophecy in Jeremiah 33 is analogous to its reappropriation of Jeremiah 23, and invites us to interpret our own experience as testimony to God's faithfulness even as we tell the truth about what has not happened yet.

Zechariah 14:4-9. The Old Testament text in the Episcopal lectionary comes from a different moment in Israel's history and approaches the task of waiting for redemption from a more radical position than does the passage from Jeremiah. The picture of God as a warrior who masses troops against the holy city and then turns in battle against those same troops is a terrible vision, a chilling alternative to the conventional God of the Christmas season who comes bearing gifts and spreading good will, or even to the God of Jeremiah 33 who continues to act redemptively before the consummation. The name Second Zechariah is often given to the writer(s) of the oracles in chapters 9–14 because their historical context is apparently later than those of the first eight chapters. Moreover, this anonymous prophet speaks of God's judgment and salvation in even starker and more realistic terms than the sixth-century Judahite responsible for the first eight chapters who gives his name to the whole book. The fifth-century prophet says that very bad news is intimately related to the good news of redemption, a stock apocalyptic theme that acknowledges that things for God's people will get much worse before they get better.

Apocalyptic texts are often particularly difficult for North Americans to preach because this attitude flatly contradicts the Western notions of "progress" that have prevailed among us since the Enlightenment. The late fifth-century prophet no longer trusts the restored temple to nurture the people's holiness and no longer looks to an increase in proper religious behavior to turn the tide of Israel's fortunes as his predecessor did (cf., for example, 1:14-17; 2:7-10; 6:12-15). The oracle concerning a "worthless shepherd" that begins in 11:17 and is later picked up in 13:7-9 suggests that the prophet also has little confidence in a restored monarchy to hold Israel together (contrast "First" Zechariah's promise of the Branch in 3:8; 6:12) and looks instead to God's cataclysmic intervention as the people's only hope. This is at the heart of what eventually becomes so characteristic of the apocalyptic literature of the second (B.C.E.) and following centuries (for instance, Daniel 7–12; the Enoch literature, 4 Ezra, 2 Baruch, and Christian writers such as Paul, Mark, Matthew, and John of Patmos).

It is a mistake, however, to characterize an apocalyptic view such as Second Zechariah's as bleak or despairing. For all its radical shape and nearly frantic tone, these revelations of God's intention for the future are designed to evoke hope. Despite the apparent triumph of sinful influences among God's people, says this prophet, God will indeed one day be king "over all the earth" and the whole human race will in unison confess Israel's *Shema*: "The Lord our God is one Lord" (Zech. 14:9; cf. Deut. 6:4). But until that day, the enemies of God—and of God's people—are indeed on the ascendance. To portray God as the general of hostile rather than friendly forces, although grotesque (cf. the terrible tortures enumerated in 14:12-15), is a way of asserting divine sovereignty in the midst of what seems to be divine defeat. For all their apparent invincibility, Israel's enemies are but tools in the hands of Israel's God.

Apocalyptic literature, even in the early and nascent form we see in Zechariah 14, always pulls its readers in the direction of solidarity with those who suffer serious discrepancies between their lived experience and their religious expectations, because these are the people who produced and first heard it. When your life contradicts your legitimate expectations, when the wicked prosper and the righteous suffer, when God's own covenant faithfulness seems to be compromised by human forces of culture or politics or economics, when evil itself goes unchecked and unpunished, there are several responses available. You can relinquish your expectations as unrealistic and recast your image of God into a more manageable deity whose reduced sovereignty is not so likely to disappoint. You can even dispense with confidence in God altogether, as with a delusion or a pipe dream. Alternatively, you can reshape your convictions about God's love for the world and the covenant people to make room for defeat and disaster as either punishment for sin or education for virtue. Each of these possibilities holds a measure of appeal and, from antiquity to the present, people have used them to make religious sense of their lives.

The apocalypticist, however, persists in maintaining both the confidence that God is able and inclined to keep covenant faith and the conviction that the community's experience of pain (whether physical, social, economic, or psychic) is an affront to God as well as to the people themselves. A seer like Second Zechariah says God's way of accounting takes seriously the suffering of the present moment and gives it redemptive meaning rather than relativizing, redefining, or diminishing it. To say that only God is able to right the wrongs of the present age, that human efforts at justice—no matter how sincere or well organized or clever—are finally inadequate, that this world is insufficient to restore health and wholeness, can be a risky venture, since to do so might encourage passivity or despair. But Jewish apocalyptic hope invariably carries with it moral exhortation, a call to repentance, and a vision of renewed holiness among those who stand in the presence of the Holy One (cf. the conclusion of the vision in 14:20-21).

From the prophet's perspective, it is the oneness of God that demands the unity of creation's worship, rather than a chauvinistic urge to impose Israel's culture and religion on its neighbors, although the violence of the apocalyptic scenario easily obscures that fact for modern Western church people. This is yet another factor that makes preaching an apocalyptic text difficult. We look a bit askance at an ancient people that experiences religious oppression or cultural marginalization and longs for a day of vengeance against its enemies. We cringe at what seems to be the prophet's contempt for cultural diversity and religious pluralism. We are easily embarrassed by the grotesque imagery of apocalyptic literature, not only because it seems primitive, but also because it seems so appallingly intolerant or arrogant.

It may be that our incapacity as moderns for empathy with an ancient seer in this regard is a function of our lack of experience on the margins more than substantive religious differences between then and now. As privileged people, as those who not only exercise power in our culture but also profit from the prevailing exercise of power by others, any similar claim from us that God will be on our side, punish those who oppose us, and bring the rest of the world around to our way of thinking would indeed be intolerant and arrogant. From the vantage point of the powerless, however—the perspective of the prophet and his original hearers—the call for vengeance and longing for the whole world's confession of Israel's God function to maintain trust in God in the midst of terrible assaults on God's integrity.

The picture in vv. 4-5 of God whose enormous feet split the mountain signals the cosmic—not only the religious or social or political—significance of God's coming restoration. The King of all the earth is the Creator of it, which means that creation itself is the locus of God's redemptive activity, not simply the backdrop to it. How easy it is for North Americans, who have both a religious and a civic heritage of exalted individualism, to rest comfortable with a gospel that addresses only human souls in need of saving without also hearing its social, political, economic, and ecological dimensions. The disorientation of Advent ought to result in discontent with things as they are in the church and in the world, including particularly our complicity in economic structures that jeopardize the earth as well as its inhabitants.

SECOND LESSON: 1 THESSALONIANS 3:9-13

Timothy's report on the Thessalonian congregation's welfare (see 3:6, which is really the beginning of the pericope) elicits from the apostle praise and thanksgiving to God. Throughout the letter, Paul mentions the Thessalonians' faith and love as evidence of their well-being, the product of their having heard the gospel he preached "not in word only, but also in power and in the Holy Spirit and with full conviction" (1:5). The triad of virtues "faith, hope, and love" so familiar from the later 1 Corinthians 13 appears already at 1 Thess. 1:3 and 5:8, and although "hope" is not explicitly named with "faith" (vv. 6, 7, 9) and "love" (vv. 6, 12) in this passage, hope's object is its focus: "the coming of our Lord Jesus" (v. 13). The apostle's prayer for his flock is that God will build on the strength of its faith, hope, and love so that it will be prepared for the Lord's return in glory (3:13).

Christian hope receives its shape from its content. The character of hopeful living is drawn not from a human attitude of cheerfulness or an optimistic stance toward life but instead from the nature of God's action in raising Jesus from the dead. Christian hope begins, therefore, with the reality of the cross, not with wishful thinking about the future. Consequently, the hopeful Christian life is founded on God's love that is made known in the cross of Christ and that is evidenced in the apostle's love for his congregation and their love for one another (v. 12) and for him (v. 6).

Preparation for the coming of the Lord is quite concrete from Paul's perspective: he prays that God will strengthen their hearts in *holiness* so that they might be blameless at the Lord's parousia, that time when, he says elsewhere, God "will judge the secret thoughts of all" (Rom. 2:16). The motif of judgment that runs through Zechariah's oracle is thus here in 1 Thessalonians as well. Holiness for Paul, as for Jews generally, is what is required of human beings who stand in God's presence, as the biblical refrain exhorts, "You must be holy because I am holy" (Lev. 11:45).

There are two conventional ways of construing that holiness in the Old Testament: in terms of purity that is maintained in largely personal and individual ways (for instance, by avoiding contact with *im*purity), or in terms of corporate and communal justice that is maintained by right relationships. The former is characteristic of such books as Leviticus, Ezra, and Nehemiah; the latter is found more in prophets like Amos or Second Isaiah. Although Paul is at points concerned with the maintenance of Christians' purity, notably with regard to sexual behavior (1 Thess. 4:1-8; cf. 1 Cor. 5:1-13), he much more frequently enjoins holiness as righteousness or justice (the same original is translated with either word, in both Hebrew and Greek), specifically as that is demonstrated in the church's life together. As here in 1 Thessalonians, elsewhere Paul says the community's holiness is manifested in its mutual love, forbearance, unity, and faithfulness (cf. Rom. 11:16; 12:1; 1 Cor. 3:17; 2 Cor. 6:14-17). Paul describes "blamelessness" at Phil. 2:15 as the community's being free of murmuring or arguing, and at 1 Thess. 2:10 he says his preaching of the gospel free of charge marks his own behavior as blameless in relationship to the Thessalonian congregation.

Preparation in Advent is therefore marked by the pursuit and maintenance of the church's holiness, in order that it may be blameless at the day of the Lord's return. This offers a good opportunity to reflect on the character of corporate righteousness rather than focusing on personal piety or purity. The church's justice is threatened not only by what the liturgy calls its "unhappy divisions" or by blatant demonstrations of its injustice toward those marginalized by racism, economic disadvantage, or differences from mainstream lifestyles, but also by its fear and self-protection in the face of daunting challenges. As the cultural disestablishment of American Protestantism becomes increasingly evident, the dwindling numbers and resources and influence of congregations and denominations often elicit urgent exhortations to recapture past victories and return to former glories. But Paul reminds the Thessalonians that the church's life is "destined" (v. 3) for struggle, not exempted from it. Persecutions in the first century (or waning cultural influence in the twentieth century) are part and parcel of Christian experience rather than disconfirmations of it. In 2 Cor. 1:3-7, Paul links the afflictions of the apostolic mission and its congregations directly to Christ's suffering to say that those who by baptism share Christ's identity also share his destiny—both his suffering and his vindication by God. That is what the cruciform life looks like. Paul's later interpreter, the writer of Colossians, takes the thought a step further to say that the church's suffering actually "complet[es] what is lacking in Christ's afflictions" (Col. 1:24). We frequently think of suffering as that which happens to other people, especially people outside the church or beyond the security of our communities. Here the apostle says that suffering—willing, voluntary suffering with and on behalf of others—is a defining characteristic of the church, a necessary consequence of faithfulness to God in a broken and fallen world.

Paul prays for the church's blamelessness in preparation for the Lord's return. This calls for pursuit of authentic holiness in the congregation, the maintenance of faithfulness in the face of hardship (cf. 1 Thess. 3:1-5), and genuine love for one another (v. 12). The unfinished character of redemption is as evident in the church as it is in the world. For all the warmth of Paul's gratitude for the Thessalonian church's life, he nevertheless prays that he will be granted another visit with them in order that he might "restore whatever is lacking in your faith" (v. 10). He worries that their experience of hostility from their neighbors might erode their confidence in God's trustworthiness, which is one way of saying what Paul thinks "faith" is.

Finally, the apostle may have one eye on the world beyond the congregation in this part of his letter that speaks so intimately of his relationship with the congregation. He prays for the increase of their love "for one another *and for all*" (v. 12). The church that is called into being by God's love is to be conformed to that love as it is made known in the cross of Christ. Indeed, Paul will in a later paragraph remind them that they have literally been "taught by God" how to love (4:9-10). The phrase "and for all" in 3:12 may refer to "all the brothers and sisters," that is, all Christians, but it may also refer to the cruciform lifestyle that reflects God's love for the entire world. In Rom. 5:6-8 Paul says in the strongest possible terms that God's love for us precedes our response to it. Although he customarily calls believers to love one another rather than to love outsiders (cf., for example, the attitude displayed in 1 Cor. 5:9-13), it is at least conceivable that here in 1 Thessalonians he envisions the congregation's mutual love and its love for the other Christian communities in the Pauline mission to have a still broader manifestation in love for the world.

GOSPEL: LUKE 21:25-36; 19:28-40

Luke 21:25-36. In each cycle of the lectionary, the First Sunday in Advent includes a portion of Jesus' apocalyptic discourse (also found in Mark 13 and Matthew 24–25) to underline the element of expectation that marks the season. The church year thus begins not with the beginning of the story of Jesus, but with the beginning of the story of the end, yet another reminder that Christians experience time in a way that upsets the normal secular reckoning. Luke's particular version of the discourse fits rather neatly with the morning's text from Jeremiah, for Luke also envisions God's coming redemption from the perspective of God's present active involvement with the church and the world.

Much of the first part of the pericope (Luke 21:25-33) is drawn directly from Mark 13:24-32, and Luke's few alterations of it are telling. First, whereas Mark casts Jesus' revelations about the end time as private instruction on the Mount of Olives granted to only four of his disciples (Mark 13:3), Luke sets the scene in the Temple itself (21:1-4) and addresses Jesus' words to a crowd that includes but is not limited to the Twelve. Second, Luke arranges and edits what he reads in Mark 13 to make a very clear point about the sequence of events to come and to make room in the eschatological scenario for the life and mission of the church.

Luke's Jesus predicts both the destruction of the Temple and of the holy city (21:5-24) in language greatly reminiscent of Mark 13, but with critical differences. The disciples in Luke ask not "when *all* these things will be completed" (Mark 13:4, referring specifically to the Temple's destruction), but "when this is about to happen" (Luke 21:7), suggesting that, as horrible as it is to contemplate, the Temple's destruction is not itself part of the eschatological drama. So also, the false preachers in Mark say only "I am he," meaning "I am the Messiah" (Mark 13:6), whereas in Luke they say also "the time has drawn near" (Luke 21:8). A premature announcement of the end time is thereby labeled not merely unwise but false prophecy. Luke further emphasizes the delay of the end in 21:9 by adding "first" to the prediction of wars and changing Mark's "not yet" to "not immediately" and inserting a temporal reference at 21:12, "before all these things," that rearranges Mark's chronology significantly. The time of the church's persecution and faithful witness detailed in Luke 21:12-19 thus *precedes* the time of cosmic distress, war, and famine that signals the end. Most notably, Luke adds an element not present in Mark's prediction of the last things, the domination of Jerusalem by the Gentiles (21:24; see John T. Carroll, *Response to the End of History: Eschatology and Situation in Luke-Acts* [SBLDS 92; Atlanta: Scholars Press, 1988], 103–17).

The passage for the morning continues this tendency to enumerate the stages of the end time and to focus on the pastoral needs of the church. Luke reduces Mark's very traditional description of the cosmic events that herald the eschaton (Mark 13:24-25) to a brief "there will be signs in sun and moon and stars" (v. 25a), and he then adds a graphic depiction of human beings' experiences of those cosmic events: nations will know distress and perplexity, people will faint with fear and foreboding (vv. 25b-26). Luke's emphasis, as distinct from Mark's, is on people's experience rather than on the heavenly portents themselves. Most significantly, Luke changes the plural "clouds" on which Mark's Son of Man will arrive (Mark 13:26, an apparent allusion to the picture in Dan. 7:13) to a single "cloud" and deletes altogether Mark's picture of the accompanying angels and gathering of the elect from the ends of the earth (Mark 13:27; cf. Zech. 2:6). This coming of the Son of Man in Luke is thus not the final one that will usher in the eschatological conditions. For Luke, this is but the beginning of the final drama, not its conclusion. Pay attention when you see this, he says to the church, "because your redemption is drawing near" (21:28), even though it is not yet present. This coming of the Son of Man is not yet the parousia that will inaugurate the judgment and the celebration of God's reign (alluded to in 21:36) but for those who trust God it is nevertheless a sure sign that salvation is near.

Underlining this point is Luke's alteration of Mark 13:29. He changes Mark's "when you see these things taking place, you know that *he* is near, at the very gates" to "when you see these things taking place, you know that the *kingdom of God* is near" (Luke 21:31). What is near for Luke is the "kingdom" rather than the Son of Man, since in Luke God's realm is in large measure already present in the believing community even before Jesus' parousia brings its fullness. Luke 17:20-21 illustrates the point: "Once Jesus was asked by the Pharisees when the kingdom of God was coming, and he answered, 'The kingdom of God is not coming with things that can be observed; nor will they say, "Look, here it is!" or "There it is!" For, in fact, the kingdom of God is among you.'" Similarly, in his charge to the seventy, Jesus instructs the missionaries to preach, "the kingdom of God has come near to you" (10:9) and in his interpretation of his own ministry of exorcism, he assures the crowd that challenges him, "if it is by the finger of God that I cast out demons, then the kingdom of God has come to you" (11:20).

Jesus' exhortations to watch in 21:34-36 include a typically Lukan moral component: do not become distracted by wild living or anxiety (v. 34) and pray that you will have strength to escape and to withstand temptation (v. 36). Postponement of the end does not mean for Luke the elimination of it, by any means. For Luke, Jesus' parousia and the full revelation of God's dominion are surely imminent even if they are not quite as immediate as some other early Christians—Paul and Mark, for example—describe them as being. Luke's theological innovation in this regard is to preserve the church's hope in God's future restoration even as he extends the heavenly schedule to provide a period of time for the life and work of the church itself. Much as Jeremiah's interpreter makes room in the divine economy for the present experience of the people of God before the end, so Luke also pays careful attention to the present life of the church as it awaits the fullness of its redemption. His exhortation is not only to watch and wait, but to work.

Luke 19:28-40. Luke's story of Jesus' so-called triumphal entry into Jerusalem also follows Mark closely, except in a few telling places. The disciples set Jesus on the donkey rather than Jesus sitting on the beast himself (Luke 19:35; cf. Mark 11:7), which suggests that the disciples self-consciously invoke the images from Zech. 9:9 of the triumphant king who leads a victory procession home from battle. As in Mark, so in Luke the description of the people who throw their garments down before Jesus calls to mind the story in 2 Kings 9:13 of Jehu's officers who do the same for the general after Elisha anoints him king. So also the crowd in Luke shouts, "Blessed is the *king* who comes in the name of the Lord," which expands Mark's "Blessed is the *one* who comes. . . ." Luke thus makes explicit what is implicit in Mark's story and develops it. There is an ironic quality to Mark's story, since only to the reader does Jesus appear to be a victorious king riding into his capital. The characters in the story—including, it seems, even the hapless disciples—think Jesus is merely a festival-goer like themselves, so they greet one another with the traditional words of Ps. 118:26, "Hosanna! Blessed is the one who comes in the name of the LORD!" Or perhaps it would be better to render their words, "Blessed in the name of the LORD is the one who comes," that is, the one who comes to the holy city to celebrate the feast. The crowd in Mark also rejoices in "the coming kingdom of our ancestor David" (11:10), which on the level of the narrative gives voice to conventional hopes for national renewal, but on the level of Mark's theological interpretation of events ironically identifies Jesus' arrival in Jerusalem to be crucified as the inauguration of the reign of God, even though the characters in the story remain blind to the fact.

In Luke's version of the story, however, the crowd no longer shouts in the recognizable words of the Psalm, words that are familiar from other festival processions, but directly identifies Jesus as the Messiah: "Blessed is the king who comes in the name of the Lord!" (Luke 19:38). Luke thus removes the ambiguity from Mark's story and eliminates the element of irony. This is quite in keeping with his earlier stories that demonstrate how easily people recognize Jesus and understand the implications of his identity as Messiah. Even before Jesus is born, the (also unborn) John rejoices in the presence of the one his mother Elizabeth calls "my Lord" (1:43). At Jesus' birth, angels proclaim him Savior and Messiah (2:11). Simeon recognizes in the infant Jesus the one in whom God would deliver "the redemption of Jerusalem" (2:38). The phrase "peace in heaven and glory in the highest" the crowd shouts in 19:38 reprises the angels' song from 2:14 and suggests that the people remember (or at least discern) what the heavenly messengers announced at Jesus' birth.

The Pharisees' rebuke to Jesus in v. 39, "order your disciples to stop," is similar to the opponents' challenge in Matt. 21:16, "do you hear what these are saying?" although it is more strongly worded. Jesus' response in Luke, however, speaks not of "infants and nursing babes" who praise God (Matt. 21:16 = Ps. 8:2), but of the very stones that would cry out were the human beings to be silenced (Luke 19:40). This picture of the earth joining in the praise of God foreshadows the later apocalyptic signs that will be described in chapters 21–22, and says that the whole universe is affected by the coming of the king—not just a particular human or political reality. The earth itself would bless Jesus if people were prevented from doing so. The cosmic upheaval detailed in Zechariah is thus deliberately alluded to here, particularly in light of the story's geographical setting on the Mount of Olives (Luke 19:29; cf. Zech. 14:4). To those with eyes to see, the king of all the earth is riding in triumph into his capital city. To those hostile to him, Luke says, Jesus is merely an embarrassing pretender who has rowdy and ill-mannered supporters. Luke, as Zechariah, knows the dual nature of the Word of God that invariably comes as bad news for some and good news for others and therefore always elicits a divided response.

Second Sunday in Advent

Lectionary	First Lesson	Psalm	Second Lesson	Gospel
Revised Common	Bar. 5:1-9 or Mal. 3:1-4	Luke 1:68-79	Phil. 1:3-11	Luke 3:1-6
Episcopal (BCP)	Bar. 5:1-9	Psalm 126	Phil. 1:1-11	Luke 3:1-6
Roman Catholic	Bar. 5:1-9	Ps. 126:1-6	Phil. 1:4-6, 8-11	Luke 3:1-6
Lutheran (LBW)	Mal. 3:1-4	Psalm 126	Phil. 1:3-11	Luke 3:1-6

FIRST LESSON: MALACHI 3:1-4; BARUCH 5:1-9

Malachi 3:1-4. The lectionary passage is taken from the middle of the fourth of six debates that make up the book of Malachi (1:2-5; 1:6—2:9; 2:10-16; 2:17—3:5; 3:6-12; 3:13—4:3). In each debate, God or the prophet makes an indictment of the degraded state of life and worship in the postexilic community, after which the priests or the people respond to the charge, and God answers. In this section, the prophet opens (2:17a) with the frightening observation that God is tired of listening to the people. This judgment is provoked by the false claims quoted in v. 17b that God does not vindicate the suffering. It is not clear whether these are the despairing words of sufferers who have lost hope or the cynical claims of those who have lost faith. But in either case, the response from God is a promise that "my messenger" will come to reform temple worship and restore just community relationships.

The specific crimes enumerated in v. 5 are both cultic and communal in nature, and several recall specific provisions of the Decalogue. Sorcerers invoke divine powers that rightly belong only to God, but they also do so at the expense of those who pay exorbitant prices for their services. Adultery, false witness, and oppression of the marginalized (laborers, widows, orphans, and aliens) do violence to community bonds, but they are also evidence, says Malachi, of disdain for the LORD of Hosts. Right religion issues in right relationships, he says, or else its orthodoxy is a sham and is subject to the same judgment God levels against the pagans. Until offerings are presented by God's people within a context of justice they do not and cannot please God.

Malachi rails against careless worship and corrupt social practices, but retains a measure of confidence that renewed worship can restore the nation's fortunes. The coming of the day of the LORD, however, is bad news before it is good news, much as it is in Second Zechariah's visions, so renewal will not come without a price. The dual metaphor of smelting ore and bleaching cloth in 3:2 uses harsh images for reform and renewal. As the raging heat of a furnace melts precious metals so that impurities can be removed or a fuller's strong soap leeches the color from fabric, so the messenger of the covenant will purify the temple priesthood in preparation for the arrival of God (3:1).

Who is this messenger? Is it an angel, since the word can be translated this way as easily as "messenger"? Is the messenger perhaps a priest or a prophet? The name "Malachi" given to this book of prophecy translates the words "my messenger" and the description of a legitimate priest in 2:7 calls him "a messenger of the LORD of Hosts." The identity of the purifying messenger in Malachi remains ambiguous, which has invited both Jews and Christians over time to speculate.

Contemporary Christians often assume the messenger is Jesus, largely because of some creative interpretation by the composer Georg Friedrich Handel who used the passage in his oratorio *The Messiah*. Handel quotes Mal. 3:1 from the King James Version which reads, in part, "The LORD, whom ye seek, will suddenly come to His temple, even the messenger of the covenant, whom ye delight in; behold, He shall come, saith the LORD of Hosts." By rendering as a single sentence what the NRSV divides in two, the KJV gives the impression that "the LORD, whom ye seek" is the same person as "the messenger of the covenant, whom ye delight in." Furthermore, because Handel drops the first half of Mal. 3:1, which clearly distinguishes the messenger from the God who will send him to prepare people for the divine visitation, he reinforces that impression. The succeeding recitative, aria, and chorus (all from Mal. 3:1-3) strongly imply that the one whose coming is promised is the Messiah, even though that thought is utterly absent from Malachi. Handel further buttresses his interpretation by preceding the selection from Malachi with Hag. 2:6-7a in the recitative. The KJV translation of those words promises that God "will shake all nations and the desire of all nations shall come" (Hag. 2:7a). Although in context Haggai assures Zerubbabel the governor and Joshua the priest that the Gentile nations will eventually bring wealth or tribute—the NRSV reads "treasure"—into the rebuilt temple in Jerusalem, the KJV translation "desire" allows Handel the interpretive possibility that what will come to the temple is something (or someone) other than money. So also, Handel follows the chorus from Malachi, "And He Shall Purify," with the recitative "Behold, A Virgin Shall Conceive," which draws on the same sign in Isa. 7:14 that Matthew takes to be a prophecy of Jesus' birth (Matt. 1:23). The result is a picture—particularly in popular piety, which is where music and art sometimes make their greatest impressions—of Malachi's prophecy of the messenger being attached to Jesus the Messiah.

Early Jewish interpreters of Malachi and the earliest Christians, on the other hand, connected the messenger in Mal. 3:1 with the later prediction in Mal. 4:5-6 of the return of the prophet Elijah to be the forerunner of God's redemption. Sirach, for example (which is also called Ecclesiasticus), a wisdom writing from the second century B.C.E., quotes from Mal. 4:6 when it says of Elijah, "At the appointed time, it is written, you are destined to calm the wrath of God before it breaks out in fury, to turn the hearts of parents to their children, and to restore the tribes of Jacob" (Sir. 48:10). At least as early as Mark's Gospel, perhaps no more than a generation after the first Easter, a Christian writer introduces the Baptist with Malachi's words about the messenger (although he attributes them to Isaiah; Mark 1:2) and portrays John as wearing the clothing of Elijah (Mark 1:6; cf. 2 Kings 1:8) and preaching a message of repentance like that ascribed to Elijah in Malachi 4. Mark again underlines his identification of John with Elijah in 9:9ff., when, following the transfiguration (during which Jesus appears with Elijah and Moses; 9:4), Jesus explains that "Elijah has come, and they did to him whatever they pleased" (9:13). Matthew only makes explicit what is implicit in Mark's story here by adding, "Then the disciples understood that he was speaking to them of John the Baptist" (Matt. 17:13). Although Luke apparently removes Mark's description of the Baptist's Elijah-like attire from his story (Luke 3:3) and eliminates altogether Mark 9:11-13 from his narrative, he nevertheless uses Malachi's words to call John the messenger who prepares the way for Jesus (7:27). The angel Gabriel promises John's father Zechariah that the child will go before the Lord God "with the spirit and power of Elijah" (Luke 1:16-17) and he quotes Malachi's description of Elijah when he says John will "turn the hearts of parents to their children" (Luke 1:17; Mal. 4:6; cf. Sir. 48:10).

Whatever the interpreter decides is the identity of the messenger in Malachi—an angelic being, a priest or prophet from the prophet's own time, Elijah *redivivus*, or John the Baptist—the commission given the messenger is clear. He is to root out causes of injustice from God's priests in order that the people's worship might be acceptable to God. The question "Who shall stand?" in Mal. 3:2 is not merely rhetorical, designed to highlight the seriousness of the change of life required of those who would stand before God, but calls for substantive examination of personal and corporate life.

Baruch 5:1-9. The passage is not properly a prophetic oracle of salvation, despite its strong reminiscences of Second Isaiah, but is rather part of a poem of consolation (4:5—5:9) that describes the restoration of Jerusalem and the return of the exiles, most likely from the perspective of the early second century B.C.E. It draws its inspiration from Isa. 40:1, "Comfort, O comfort my people, says your God" (cf. "Take courage," Bar. 4:5, 21, 27, 30), and explains that the exile had a salutary, atoning purpose. "It was not for destruction that you were sold to the nations, but you were handed over to your enemies because you angered God" (Bar. 4:6). Despite Israel's punishment for its sin, God will restore the penitent people, their ultimate renewal will serve as a witness to the nations of God's faithfulness, and the elect will be vindicated when God destroys their enemies: "For as the neighbors of Zion have now seen your capture, so they will see your salvation by God, which will come to you with great glory and with the splendor of the Everlasting. My children, endure with patience the wrath that has come upon you from God. Your enemy has overtaken you, but you will see their destruction and will tread upon their necks" (4:24, 25).

The structure of Bar. 4:30—5:9, the second half of the poem, is marked by repeated calls for hope and comfort that have warrants in God's actions. The people should take courage from the reversal of fortunes that is at hand because God will turn the tables on Israel's enemies (4:35). They should watch for signs of vindication and plan for the celebration for God will rename the city "Righteous Peace, Godly Glory" (5:4; or: "Glory of Godliness"). They should prepare for the return of the exiles for God will personally escort them home in a victory parade (5:6, 7, 9). The exiles were driven away on foot but they will be carried back by God's own hand "as on a throne." The words of comfort draw repeatedly from Isaiah's similar offers of solace. Baruch 5:1-2, with its invitation to take off mourning clothes and put on "the beauty of the glory of God" calls to mind Isa. 61:3, "to give them a garland instead of ashes." The new name of the holy city, "Righteous Peace, Godly Glory" in Bar. 5:4 is reminiscent of Isa. 60:14 in which a restored Jerusalem is called "the City of the LORD, the Zion of the Holy One of Israel," or Isa. 62:4 where the names are "My Delight Is in Her" and "Married." "Arise O Jerusalem" in Bar. 5:5 echoes "Lift up your eyes all around and see" in Isa. 49:18, and the picture in Bar. 5:7 of mountains and hills made low and valleys filled up for Israel to travel safely home seems to draw on both the people's preparation for God in Isa. 40:4 ("every valley shall be lifted up, and every mountain and hill be made low") and God's turning "the rough places into level ground" for the homecoming of the exiles in Isa. 42:16ff.

Baruch details the work of preparation for salvation in the context of the people's current experience of defeat and despair. Although written in a postexilic context, the author takes as his pseudonym the name of one of the most well known exiles, the scribe of Jeremiah, because he considers himself and his people to be living in yet another time of exile, this one more cultural and religious perhaps than territorial. The people this time are surrounded by hostile forces that may or may not be violent, depending on whether the book is dated to the period of Seleucid or Roman domination, but are nonetheless contemptuous of the people's attempts at covenant faithfulness. To change one's clothes, as Baruch exhorts, to remove one's funeral garments (5:1) and replace them with wedding clothes (5:2), is to act out of confidence in God's future rather than to rely only on what one sees in the present. An old rabbinic maxim says that when a funeral procession and a wedding procession meet at an intersection, the wedding party should be given the right-of-way because death must always give way to life and despair bow to hope when God is in charge. To begin to live in God's future, even before that future is present, requires the courage that Baruch urges, and recalls—although obviously with a very different tone—the prophet Jeremiah's exhortation to build houses, plant gardens, and raise families in Babylon, because God has promised that the exiles will find their welfare in the welfare of the city where God has sent them (Jer. 29:7). Baruch urges hopeful action rather than hopeful thought or wishful thinking, and he calls on his contemporaries to remember that God did in fact restore those former exiles and to trust that God may similarly be trusted with their current experience of alienation.

SECOND LESSON: PHILIPPIANS 1:3-11

This passage constitutes the thanksgiving period that, following the greeting, always sets the agenda in Paul's letters for the issues that he will address in the body of the letter. In Philippians, the thanksgiving reflects the warm and loving relationship the apostle has with this congregation, as he gives thanks for their financial gift to him and their emotional support of him in a time of trouble. He writes from prison (1:7), probably in Ephesus, a city which would account both for Paul's references to imperial officials (1:13; 4:22) and for the apparent ease with which the Philippian congregation has been able to communicate with him.

Paul's gratitude to God is for the congregation's willingness to enter into partnership with him and his apostolic co-workers. The term "partnership" in antiquity reflects, as it often does today, the realm of commerce. Although the Greek word *koinonia* has taken on spiritualized meaning in Christian theology and is now often used in church circles to refer loosely to warm relationships between Christian friends or the "fellowship" of ecclesiastical social events, it stands in Paul's letters as a translation of the

Latin *societas*, a uniquely Roman sort of business agreement. A *societas* was a partnership protected by the courts although not always written as are modern corporate contracts, and entered into consensually by various parties for their mutual benefit. In forming a *societas*, people consented to share the labor and expenses of an endeavor and to profit from it together. Partners would individually contribute physical labor, money, property, social status (a commodity of no small value in Greco-Roman society), or professional skill, but all would share in the profits gained, and regardless of individuals' social or familial status, the members of a *societas* were legally regarded as equals in the context of the joint venture. Even slaves, who otherwise had no legal standing, could be partners in *societates*. Each partner was legally bound to seek the good of the partnership and forbidden to seek personal gain at its expense or that of another partner. The partnership endured so long as partners were "of the same mind" about their common goal, sharing the same purposes that originally brought the partnership into being. Paul uses the vocabulary of the *societas* in Philippians repeatedly after claiming in 1:5 to have this legal contract of consensual partnership with the congregation, most notably in 2:1-11 where he exhorts them to "be of the same mind" (v. 2) with one another and with Christ Jesus himself (v. 5) (J. Paul Sampley, *Pauline Partnership in Christ: Christian Community and Commitment in Light of Roman Law* [Philadelphia: Fortress Press, 1980], 11–17).

For Paul, partnership in the gospel (the NRSV's "sharing" in Phil. 1:5, 7 is really too bland to convey the dynamism of the concept) means shared money and material resources, such as the Philippians' financial support of him, but also shared suffering. "All of you share in God's grace with me," he says, "both in my imprisonment and in the defense and confirmation of the gospel" (1:7). Solidarity is a mark of the church, which means that even the apostolic mission itself is not a matter of Paul's individual endeavor but a product of the whole church's faithfulness. The Philippians share this mission with Paul by their support of him and their suffering with him and with each other. His specific prayer for them is that their love will continue to grow with knowledge and full insight, which means Paul recognizes what we all know about love: sometimes it is neither wise nor discerning. The reason Paul prays the Philippians will grow in love is in order that they might "test and find reliable the things that really matter," what the NRSV renders somewhat colorlessly "determine what is best" (1:10).

What God has begun in the Philippian Christians will in fact be completed at the "day of Christ" (1:6, 10) because it is God who will bring it to completion. For all the intimacy and joy in this pastoral relationship, and for all that Paul praises the congregation for its love and faithfulness, the

SECOND SUNDAY IN ADVENT

church is still moving toward a conclusion. It has not yet arrived at its destination. He wants them to continue to overflow with God's love in order that on the day of Christ they might be "pure and blameless" (1:10). "Blamelessness" as he uses it here is related to "tripping" or "causing to fall down." They will be blameless at the judgment if they do not derail the church. Love with knowledge and discernment is shown not by warm feelings but by wise actions. This blamelessness is equated with being filled with the fruits of righteousness, which recalls his language in Galatians 5 about the fruit of the Spirit, "love, joy, peace, patience, kindness, generosity, faithfulness, gentleness, and self-control" (5:22-23).

GOSPEL: LUKE 3:1-6

Some earlier study of Luke treated this passage as if it were the true beginning of the Gospel, and the birth and infancy narratives of chapters 1 and 2 were either late additions or an artificial preface to the "real" story Luke intended to tell. Although such a view is now rightly discredited, there is good reason to understand why an interpreter might have drawn such an impression. The sixfold location of the preaching of John the Baptist in so-called secular history in the first two verses parallels other prophetic introductions in the Bible (for instance, Jer. 1:1-3; Ezek. 1:1-3; Hos. 1:1; Isa. 1:1). Luke establishes the inauguration of John's public career in the context of the imperial (Tiberius) and regional (Pilate, Herod, Philip, and Lysanius) administrations of the day as well as the tenure of the high priests Annas and Caiaphas. It is the latter that prevents Luke's timeline from being described merely as "secular," of course, and points up the subtlety of the evangelist's much-vaunted theology of history. Although it is quite true that without Luke-Acts the New Testament would say nothing about the Roman emperors who ruled during the birth of the church, it is not only the civil authorities involved in the story who interest Luke. It is probably more helpful to say that in the Third Gospel we encounter a concern to locate the origins of Christianity on a global scale than a desire to relate sacred and secular, a modern distinction that would likely have been puzzling to a first-century writer. By saying that "the word of God came to John" (3:2) at this particular, recognizable moment in history, Luke deliberately recalls for the reader other critical moments when God intervened in the people's life by summoning a prophet. Jeremiah in particular received such a call to speak on God's behalf at a moment of national crisis (Jer. 1:1-4).

Luke summarizes the Baptist's preaching, much as Mark does, as "a baptism of repentance for the forgiveness of sins" (3:3) and, also with

Mark, identifies John as that "voice in the wilderness" of Isa. 40:3 who prepares the people for God's arrival. Luke extends the biblical quotation, though, to include Isa. 40:4-5, which has the effect of focusing our attention more on John's preaching than on his person (a move Luke also seems to make elsewhere in his two-volume work). By including Isaiah's affirmation that "all flesh shall see the salvation of God" Luke reprises the note of universalism that we have heard already in Simeon's description of Jesus as "a light for revelation to the Gentiles and for glory to [God's] people Israel" (2:32) and further testifies to the truth of the angels' announcement that Jesus is the savior whose birth is "good news of great joy for all the people" (2:10).

The parallel and interwoven annunciation, birth, and infancy narratives in chapters 1–2 have already made the point that John is Jesus' forerunner, so the Baptist is well prepared for when he arrives in chapter 3 as an adult. John is the "prophet of the Most High" (1:76) who proclaims the "son of the Most High" (1:32).

Third Sunday in Advent

Lectionary	First Lesson	Psalm	Second Lesson	Gospel
Revised Common	Zeph. 3:14-20	Isa. 12:2-6	Phil. 4:4-7	Luke 3:7-18
Episcopal (BCP)	Zeph. 3:14-20	Psalm 85 or 85:7-13 or Canticle 9	Phil. 4:4-7, (8-9)	Luke 3:7-18
Roman Catholic	Zeph. 3:14-18	Isa. 12:2-6	Phil. 4:4-7	Luke 3:10-18
Lutheran (LBW)	Zeph. 3:14-18a	Isa. 12:2-6	Phil. 4:4-7, (8-9)	Luke 3:7-18

FIRST LESSON: ZEPHANIAH 3:14-18a (-20)

The setting of Zephaniah's ministry in the first two chapters of the book of prophecy that bears his name is early in the reign of Josiah (640–609 B.C.E.), but prior to or perhaps in the midst of the king's much-heralded religious reform (see 2 Kings 22–23). The prophet rails against Judah's cultic corruption and social injustice in these first two chapters and promises God's judgment and punishment. This contemporary of Jeremiah is a champion of the so-called Deuteronomic reform instituted to reverse the syncretistic practices that had crept into Judah's religious life during the reigns of Manasseh and Amon. He announces the approach of the day of the LORD (1:7, 14-18), the time when God's fierce judgment will be executed not only against the pagan nations but against God's own people. It would appear that, traditionally, the day of the LORD once carried heavy tones of chauvinism as Israel longed for God's military defeat of its enemies and the establishment of its primacy among the nations, recalling, for example, "the day of Midian" (Judges 7:25). But in the hands of the eighth-century Amos, the image is transformed into a prophetic indictment of the people themselves when he asks, "Why do you want the day of the LORD? It is darkness, not light" (Amos 5:18). Zephaniah too envisions God's arrival as a warrior to be a two-edged sword, since the battle will rage against the elect who have forsaken Yahweh as much as against outsiders.

At Zeph. 3:1-13 the subject begins to shift somewhat to a promise of the eventual restoration of Jerusalem and the preservation of a remnant (v. 13) that will survive judgment and again serve God faithfully, although that has been prepared for in earlier hints that the repentant may escape destruction and "be hidden on the day of the LORD's wrath" (2:3). The passage for the Third Sunday in Advent apparently assumes that those promises of rescue have been kept, that redemption has indeed occurred. The prophet therefore issues a call to sing for joy. The presence of the king means the city need no longer fear; the presence of God means there will be no more disaster.

The people are called to sing and rejoice (3:14) because of God's restoration of the people's fortunes. In v. 17, then, even God joins the merry-making and music: "The LORD . . . will rejoice over you with gladness . . . [and] exult over you with loud singing as on a day of festival." The fact that God rejoices at the restoration of the city, even as the people do, suggests that the prophet sees God as having similarly mourned for its subjugation. Estrangement is painful to God even as it is to God's people. Verses 18b-20 are almost certainly much later, likely postexilic, additions to the oracle that once ended with God's "loud singing as on a day of festival." They seem to have been composed to adapt it to a new situation in the people's life. The word "oppressors" in vv. 18b and 19 suggests a context of the calamity of the Babylonian siege and exile rather than the harsh suppression of pagan religious influences that attended Josiah's reform. Some critics maintain that the whole of 3:14-20 comes from that later period, but vv. 14-18a are a plausible response to the promise of God's rescue in 3:9-13. Particularly the language of v. 15, "The king of Israel, the LORD, is in your midst," recalls the language of some enthronement psalms like Ps. 47:8, "God is king over the nations; God sits on his holy throne" (cf. Psalms 68; 93; 97), and is an entirely proper response if in fact people have been delivered from faithlessness and corruption to a right covenant relationship with God. God's righteous sovereignty, God's identity as ruler, is best manifested not in the defeat of alien nations but the righteous life of God's own people. This is cause for rejoicing not only for the people but for God as well.

Christian tradition calls the Third Sunday of Advent *Gaudete* Sunday, from the Latin word for "rejoice." The liturgical color shifts for one week from purple, a mark of penitence as well as a sign of royalty, to pink, a traditional statement of joy. The waiting is half over, we say on this day, not simply because two weeks of Advent have been completed and only two remain before Christmas. The waiting for salvation too is coming to an end. Even in the midst of our life in a broken and unredeemed world, still God can be trusted to complete that which has begun in Christ, and this is cause for great joy.

SECOND LESSON: PHILIPPIANS 4:4-7, (8-9)

The theme of rejoicing is repeated in the epistle lesson. The entire letter to the Philippians resounds with descriptions of Paul's joy (1:4, 18; 2:2, 17, 19; 4:1, 10), the church's joy (1:25; 2:18, 28-29), and his exhortations to them to rejoice still more (3:1; 4:4). The combination of the apostle's personal intimacy with this congregation that supports him so steadfastly and his own expressions of delight in what he sees God doing in the gospel mission creates a tone that makes this letter (or, more likely, pieces of several letters addressed to the same people) distinctive in his extant correspondence.

Rejoice and do not worry, Paul says, because the Lord is near (4:4-5). Is this nearness spatial or temporal? Psalm 145:18 pictures God drawing physically close to those who call for help, and the language Paul uses here recalls that of the psalmist. Paul's predominant expectation, though, is of the imminent return of the risen Lord on the clouds to gather his elect (for instance, 1 Thess. 1:10). It probably does not make sense to make too great a distinction between these senses of nearness, though, for two reasons. On the one hand, Paul's conviction that God has already begun to initiate the new aeon of redemption in Jesus' death and resurrection in the midst of the old age of sin and death means that old and new at times virtually coexist. He says to the Corinthians, for example, "the appointed time has grown short" (1 Cor. 7:29), but that also means that the nearness of salvation is literally pressing in on the unredeemed world in which the church lives. "In view of the impending crisis, it is well for you to remain as you are" (1 Cor. 7:26) might well be paraphrased, "Given the palpable intrusion of the new age into the old, there is no time to change things like your marital status before the Lord's return." On the other hand, the nearer Jesus draws to the church in spatial terms—one might think here of the Spirit's presence in the community as Paul does in Rom. 8:18-27—the sooner will be his victory over the forces hostile to God. This is the reason Christians can pray with confidence that God will hear and answer (Phil. 4:5), because Jesus' nearness to the church brings the church near to God.

The peace of God will guard you, Paul says at v. 7, and he promises that "the God of peace will be with you" at v. 9. The thought here is really incomplete without vv. 8-9. God's peace, God's all-encompassing sustenance of life and generosity, what the Bible calls *shalom*, is a safeguard against forces that would threaten the church's life or shake its confidence (cf. 1:27-28). Because the church's life is, however, cruciform—shaped by the cross of Christ—and therefore marked by self-giving love even "to the point of death" (2:8), God's peace is by no means easy to understand. The conventional sense of *eirēnē* as the ceasing of hostility would be much easier to comprehend. God's peace would then mean a protection from enemies. Paul knows instead that the church struggles in the world, that its faithfulness to God results in imprisonment and hostility and suffering with and on behalf of the fallen creation. So God's peace is very much *not* the restraint of the church's enemies. This is the reason it "surpasses all understanding" (v. 7). Paul considers divine peace in terms of our reconciliation with God (cf. Rom. 5:1; 2 Cor. 5:16—6:2). God acts to end humanity's hostility by disarming the power of sin in human life. The result is "peace with God" although not necessarily peace with the part of the world that remains wedded to sin and death. When we are tempted to think of God's peace as a protection from harm or an escape from the costly demands of faithful life, we have transformed authentic *shalom* into a magic amulet.

"Keep on doing the things that you have learned" (v. 9) includes "think[ing] about" whatever is true, honorable, just, pure, pleasing (that is, to God), commendable, excellent, or praiseworthy (v. 8). The verb translated "think" is elsewhere in Paul's letters rendered "consider" or "reckon," and has less to do with contemplation or reflection than active appropriation. "Take account of these things" is another way to put it. Let these characteristics inform and shape your own behavior and life together, even as you have already done. This string of virtues, in some ways so like virtue lists found among pagan moralists, nevertheless receives a strong Christian flavor from its literary context. That which is praiseworthy, for example, is from Paul's perspective that which elicits praise from God, not from human beings (cf. Rom. 2:29). This is not speculative theology but concrete paraenesis, moral exhortation grounded in the apostle's life and preaching among them ("what you have learned and received and heard and seen *in me,*" v. 9). Elsewhere, he makes similar calls to imitate him (1 Cor. 4:16; 11:1; 1 Thess. 1:6; 2:14) but those imperatives either make explicit or imply that Paul's own imitation of Christ determines the modeling of the believer's life after apostolic life. At still other points, he calls Christians to imitate Christ directly themselves (Rom. 15:1-7; 1 Cor. 11:1; Gal. 6:2), most notably in this very letter (Phil. 2:5-11). He thinks here not of particular stories about the kindness or caring of Jesus of Nazareth that believers should emulate but of the nature of Jesus' death on the cross and what it reveals about God's love.

GOSPEL: LUKE 3:7-18

John's preaching, as Luke presents it, contains the much-heralded three points of a traditional sermon. The first (vv. 7-9) concerns the imminent eschaton and the demand for repentance in preparation for it; the second (vv. 10-14) deals with specific ethical implications of the call to repentance; and the third (vv. 15-17) proclaims the nearness of God's Messiah and a hint about what his ministry will look like.

Whereas Mark merely summarizes John's preaching as "a baptism of repentance for the forgiveness of sins" (Mark 1:4), Q describes the content of that preaching in some detail, and both Matthew (3:7-10) and Luke (3:7-9) insert it at the same point in their retellings of Mark's story. For Luke, however, John's sermon is addressed not to the scribes and Pharisees, as it is in Matthew, but to the crowds that include "all sorts and conditions" of persons, including tax collectors (3:12) and soldiers (3:14). In rather conventional Jewish religious terms, John says that authentic religion issues in just personal and community life. This conviction could as easily be found in one of the ancient biblical prophets like Amos or Hosea as in a first-century country preacher like John. But the Baptist adds apocalyptic eschatological urgency to his preaching by warning that "even now the ax is lying at the root of the trees; every tree that does not bear good fruit is cut down and thrown into the fire" (Luke 3:9). The moment of judgment is quite near, he says, and mere religious affiliation or membership in the chosen people ("we have Abraham as our ancestor," 3:8) will scarcely shield those whose fruitless lives or unjust relationships are an affront to the justice of God.

At this point, Luke expands on the Q tradition by interpreting it with a dialogue between the Baptist and his hearers. "What then should we do?" they ask, in the same words with which the Jerusalem crowd at Pentecost will later respond to Peter's sermon about Jesus (Acts 2:37). In an era when most preaching elicits polite thank-yous and variations on "It was a meaningful message, Pastor," how remarkable it seems to us for a preacher's words to evoke such a disarming—and disarmed—response. This is what Luke thinks authentic proclamation accomplishes, though: it "cuts to the heart" (Acts 2:37) and speaks directly to the most intimate parts of life. So the Baptist says to the crowd, made up most likely of people who earn barely subsistent livings, "Share what you have" (Luke 3:11).

To the often-wealthy and always-despised toll collectors who hear him, John says, "Stop making your living off the backs of your neighbors." Although tax franchises were expected—even by the Romans who sold them to the locals—to be profitable for their holders, John tells the toll collectors in his audience to gather only what they have been charged to gather and to refrain from demanding the additional moneys they were accustomed to gouging out of the populace. Whereas the poor are charged to share what little they have as demonstration of true repentance, the toll collectors must give up their opportunity to attain wealth to show they are prepared to enter the kingdom of God. In the same way, John exhorts the soldiers, who are not to be understood as Roman legions, but rather Jewish mercenaries in Herod's service, to restrain the common impulse to use their (derived) authority to shake down their neighbors for personal gain. And John further adds explicitly what may be implicit in his words to the toll collectors: "be satisfied with your wages" (3:14).

Joseph A. Fitzmyer points out the curious mix of radical ethical content and elements of what might be termed social conservatism in John's preaching (*The Gospel According to Luke I–IX* [AB 28; Garden City, N.Y.: Doubleday, 1981], 465). John says, on the one hand, that true repentance is marked by communitarian values of sharing goods and concern for one another's well-being, even to the extent of depriving oneself of potential gain. On the other hand, however, John does not tell toll collectors to sever their relationship with the Empire and cease to participate in the system of taxation, only to refrain from profiting from it personally, and he does not call mercenaries to lay down their arms, merely to stop throwing their weight around for personal advancement. Likely the most significant aspect of John's ethical teaching here is the fact that it reflects the evangelist's use of money and possessions as "a symbol of the state of a [person's] heart before God" (Luke Timothy Johnson, *The Literary Function of Possessions in Luke-Acts* [SBLDS 39; Missoula: Scholars Press, 1977], 159). Because wealth—in any amount—is so pervasive and powerful a force in human life, how one handles one's possessions is a measure of one's response to God.

The third point of John's sermon grows out of the second as the second did from the first. John's call to repentance and right living is apparently perceived by the crowd as just the preparation for the Lord's arrival that Isaiah 40 predicted and Luke 3:4-6 assured the reader was the mission of the Baptist. The people therefore are "filled with expectation" and begin to ask questions of a distinctly messianic flavor (v. 15). Here Luke continues to use the story he finds in Q, although at this point it begins to parallel Mark substantially. The Baptist contrasts his own baptism with water for repentance with the mightier one whose baptism will come with the Holy Spirit and fire. In Mark, Jesus' baptism will be only "with the Holy Spirit" while Matthew and Luke read in their source that the Spirit is attended by fire, much as it is in Isa. 4:4-5, 32:15; 44:3; Ezek. 36:25-26; Mal. 3:2b-3. John has already warned that the fire of judgment is in store for those who do not prepare for God (3:9), and the fire of the Messiah's baptism will apparently be similarly a sign of judgment and purification, since he will separate the wheat from the chaff and burn the latter "with unquenchable fire" (3:17). In the larger context of Luke's two-volume work, however, these mentions of fire, particularly in association with the Holy Spirit, prepare the way for the story of Pentecost in Acts 2, where the flames of fire signify the arrival of the Spirit on the company of Christian believers.

THIRD SUNDAY IN ADVENT

John's preaching is expressly called "preaching the gospel" in v. 18, and that is frequently taken to refer only to the last of his three points, the promise of the Messiah. It is clear, though, that Luke thinks that John's call to repentance and his ethical exhortations are every bit as much "good news" as are his words about Jesus. The same verb Luke uses to characterize the Baptist's preaching is used of the angel's proclamation to the shepherds in 2:10. At the end of Luke's story, the risen Jesus himself tells the gathered disciples that "repentance and forgiveness of sins is to be proclaimed in his name to all nations, beginning from Jerusalem" (24:47).

How is a call to repentance good news? How can a call to right living be heard as "gospel" for those in the church (particularly in its Lutheran and Reformed parts) who are habituated to opposing faith and works in the strictest of terms? For Luke, repentance and reformation are nothing less than what God has always wanted for human life. In classically Jewish terms, Luke considers right living to be the only legitimate evidence of one's trust in God; Christianity for him is the logical and necessary completion of Judaism rather than its alternative or successor. The story of the rich man and Lazarus, for example (Luke 16:19-31), concludes with the chilling refusal of "father Abraham" to send a warning from heaven to the rich man's remaining brothers to mend their ways. "They have Moses and the prophets; they should listen to them," replies Abraham, and the rich man counters, "No, father Abraham; but if someone goes to them from the dead, they will repent." Then Abraham says, with no small irony in the context of a Gospel about Jesus, "If they do not listen to Moses and the prophets, neither will they be convinced *even if someone rises from the dead*" (16:29-31). There is no difference whatsoever between what God calls for in the Law and the Prophets and what Jesus preaches on God's behalf. The terrible specificity of John's demands on the crowds, the tax collectors, and the soldiers leaves no room for religious generalities or substitutions of right doctrine for sound ethics. To prepare for the advent of the Holy One means to seek holiness oneself.

Fourth Sunday in Advent

Lectionary	First Lesson	Psalm	Second Lesson	Gospel
Revised Common	Micah 5:2-5a	Ps. 80:1-7 or Luke 1:47-55	Heb. 10:5-10	Luke 1:39-45, (46-55)
Episcopal (BCP)	Micah 5:2-4	Psalm 80 or 80:1-7	Heb. 10:5-10	Luke 1:39-49, (50-56)
Roman Catholic	Micah 5:1-4	Ps. 80:2-4, 15-16, 18-19	Heb. 10:5-10	Luke 1:39-45
Lutheran (LBW)	Micah 5:2-4	Ps. 80:1-7	Heb. 10:5-10	Luke 1:39-45, (46-55)

FIRST LESSON: MICAH 5:1-4

Chapters 4–5 of the book of Micah, although certainly inspired by the words of the working-class contemporary of the classical eighth-century prophets Isaiah of Jerusalem, Amos, and Hosea, appear to have been at least edited—and perhaps even composed—by a postexilic prophet who interprets the nation's catastrophic defeat at the hands of the Babylonians as God's judgment on infidelity and who promises God's ultimate deliverance and restoration. At the center of this section of the book are three related oracles, each beginning with the word "now": "Now why do you cry aloud?" (4:9-10); "Now many nations are assembled against you" (4:11-13); and "Now you are walled around with a wall" (5:1-5a). Each contrasts the present agony with the coming relief, the first with the image of childbirth (4:10), the second with the prospect of revenge (4:13), and the third—the longest—with an assurance that the Davidic monarchy will be restored.

The lectionary passage comes from this third "now" oracle, although the selected reading cuts off the initial verse and thus obscures the contrast between the present and the future. The siege is ongoing here, hostile troops surround the city of Jerusalem, and the battle has clearly turned for the worst, since the king is being mocked by enemy soldiers (v. 1). The picture is reminiscent of that described in 2 Kings 24:10-12 when King Jehoiachin is taken prisoner by the forces of Nebuchadnezzar. In the midst of this scene of disaster and despair, though, the Lord promises the nearby small village of Bethlehem, the hometown of the great King David, that it will once again produce a ruler worthy of the title and an honor to David's name. Ephrathah may have been the ancient name of the same town or a separate town that was absorbed into Bethlehem, but in the current context it serves to rename Bethlehem.

This promised king's "origin is from of old, from ancient days" (v. 2), which calls to mind the terms of Nathan's oracle to David in 2 Samuel 7 in

FOURTH SUNDAY IN ADVENT

which God assures him of a never-ending dynasty. As so often in Scripture, the king is called a shepherd (v. 4; cf. Jer. 23:1-4; Ezekiel 34), but the association is obviously with David, known as the shepherd king. As the Lord who is called a shepherd meets every need of the sheep (Ps. 23:1), so this promised son of David will feed his flock under the guidance and authority of God's own might, and hold the people secure and in peace.

SECOND LESSON: HEBREWS 10:5-10

The thought unit in this part of Hebrews is 10:1-10, and it is particularly essential to consider at least v. 1, which initiates the contrast between shadow and reality, when making sense of the subunit that is designated the morning epistle lesson. The whole pericope (vv. 1-10) constitutes an interpretation of Ps. 40:6-8, apparently based on the Greek translation of it in the Septuagint (in which it is Psalm 39) rather than the Hebrew. The second half of the first sentence in Hebrew reads, "but you have given me an open ear" (Ps. 40:6) while the writer of Hebrews reads "but a body you have prepared for me" (Heb. 10:5). This biblical interpretation stands in the service of a larger argument concerning the relationship between the "old" covenant and the "new" one that has been going on since 8:1 and will continue to 10:18.

This argument takes the form of a homiletical reflection on the contrasts between heaven and earth, old and new, external and internal that are inherent in Jesus' role as high priest and the initiation of God's "better . . . new covenant" (8:6, 8, 13; 9:15). According to Heb. 8:8-12, Jeremiah's ancient prophecy (Jer. 31:31-34) makes clear that God has intended all along to replace the first covenant with Israel with a new one, precisely because the first one did not—and could not—accomplish everything God intended with it. Because they are only a copy (Heb. 9:24), sketch (8:5; 9:23), and shadow (8:5) of the "true form" (10:1) of God's heavenly temple, sacrifices offered in the earthly temple by human priests must be repeated continually (10:1-3). Because they are repeated, those earthly sin offerings actually function as "reminder[s] of sin" (10:3) rather than as effective means for removing sin.

This is where Ps. 40:6-8, particularly with the critical substitution of "body" for "ears" in the Septuagint text, moves the argument in Hebrews forward. As so often in this book, the words of Scripture are taken to be words of Jesus. First, the body God has prepared for Christ is not for the offering of multiple "sacrifices and offerings" (v. 5) in which God takes no pleasure (v. 7). It is instead prepared for God's will, and God's will is that a single, effective, eternal sacrifice be made. In his obedience to God's will,

Jesus makes himself the desired offering and thus effects what the old cult could not (v. 10). Because Jesus' offering is both heavenly (that is, offered according to the true form of the cult rather than the earthly copy) and earthly at the same time (because "Christ came into the world," 10:5), the superiority of his priesthood is further established.

The homiletical significance of this passage from Hebrews for the last Sunday in Advent is that it explicitly connects the incarnation to the cross. How easily even believers succumb to the temptation rampant in our culture to romanticize the birth of Jesus and remove its scandal. If all we knew were that Jesus was born, even if we knew that in Jesus the very God of heaven joined our life, all we would have would be the mildly comforting notion that God understands our experience. The gospel, however, announces that the one who was born in Bethlehem is the one who was executed in Jerusalem. Jesus joins our life both to sanctify it by his presence and to redeem it by his death. Holy Week may feel many months far removed from the last week before Christmas, but it is very present in this Sunday's epistle lesson.

GOSPEL: LUKE 1:39-45, (46-56)

As the last Sunday in Advent is something of an emotional bridge between the anticipation of Advent and the joy of Christmas, so this passage in Luke provides the literary bridge between the two stories announcing the conceptions of John (1:5-25) and Jesus (1:26-38) and the two stories of their respective births and childhoods (1:57-80; 2:1-52). Gabriel has already linked the two infants when he identifies their mothers as relatives (1:36), and that provides a natural narrative means for the two women to meet.

The focus in this meeting of relatives who are both unexpectedly expectant—the one surprisingly so at an advanced age and the other full of the potential fruitfulness of youth—is not on the women themselves, though, but on their unborn children. Even before Elizabeth can return Mary's greeting (v. 40), her baby moves within her and she interprets this most common of the sensations of pregnancy as the baby's joy (vv. 41, 44). The movement of a fetus within its mother's body is naturally a cause for joy to the parents because it signals the imminent reality of their life together as a family. Elizabeth, however, attributes the joy to her unborn son, although it is joy she apparently also shares, because she marvels, "why has this happened to me, that the mother of my Lord comes to me?" (v. 43).

The parallels between these two remarkable pregnancies so carefully maintained in the first half of Luke's narrative now assume a clearly hierarchical relation as the one child pays *in utero* homage to the other, but this too has been prepared for in the preceding story. Whereas John is said to be "great in the sight of the Lord" (1:15) and will undertake his ministry "with the spirit and power of Elijah" (v. 17), Jesus will be the very Son of God for whom John will prepare (1:35) and he will inherit his royal ancestor David's dynasty (1:32). The relationship between these babies—even before they are born—recalls another prenatal relationship, although with a significant difference. Jacob and Esau, the twin sons of Isaac and Rebekah, fight with each other in their mother's womb, prefiguring their competition and struggle as adults (Gen. 25:22). John, however, greets Jesus with joy and his mother blesses Jesus' mother with words reminiscent of Gabriel's announcement to her. Beverly Roberts Gaventa demonstrates the telling parallels between Elizabeth's greeting of and Gabriel's annunciation to Mary (*Mary: Glimpses of the Mother of Jesus* [Columbia: University of South Carolina Press, 1995], 55):

Elizabeth	*Gabriel*
Blessed are you among women	You have found favor with God
Blessed is the fruit of your womb	You will conceive
The mother of my Lord	Son of the Most High
The child in my womb leaped for joy	The Holy Spirit will come upon you
Blessed is she who believed	Here am I, the servant of the Lord

It is not terribly remarkable, in the context of Luke's Gospel, that Elizabeth should understand what the angel has told Mary, even though she has not herself heard it, because she is "filled with the Holy Spirit" (1:41). Here she provides something of a foil to her husband Zechariah who, although he is a priest of God, when confronted with an angel's promise questions its trustworthiness (1:18). Mary, though, is the real antithesis to Zechariah, because she does trust what Gabriel says to her ("let it be to me according to your word," 1:38), which is precisely what Elizabeth recognizes about her ("blessed is she who believed that there would be a fulfillment of what was spoken to her by the Lord," 1:45). Martin Luther observes of this story that "The virgin birth is a mere trifle for God; that God should become human is a greater miracle; but most amazing of all is that this maiden should credit the announcement that she, rather than some other virgin, had been chosen to be the mother of God. . . . This is for us the hardest point, not so much to believe that He is the son of the Virgin and God himself, as to believe that this Son of God is ours" (translated and quoted by Roland H. Bainton from Luther's sermons in *The Martin Luther*

Christmas Book [Philadelphia: Fortress Press, 1948], 23). Augustine puts it another way when he says that Mary conceived the Christ child in her heart as much as she conceived him in her womb, thus providing the models for Christians too to conceive him in our hearts.

Mary's response to Elizabeth's blessing of her is to bless God in the words of a song (1:46-55) that bears great similarity to the song of another surprised mother, Hannah (1 Sam. 1:1-2), and draws language and imagery from throughout the Hebrew Bible. By identifying herself as God's slave (the translation "servant" is far too pallid to convey the sense of the original), first in her response to Gabriel (1:38) and second in her song of praise (1:48), Mary exhibits the classic behavior of a disciple: obedience. She expresses boundless confidence that God's promises can be trusted and are even now, in her own experience, being kept. Mary's trust in God and her recognition that God's redemption brings a dramatic reversal of prevailing values ("scattered the proud . . . brought down the powerful . . . lifted up the lowly . . . filled the hungry . . . sent the rich away," 1:51-53) identifies her as the archetypal disciple in Luke's Gospel. She believes that God's prior faithfulness to Israel has again been manifested in her own experience and can be trusted also to take the side of all who are in need.

The Nativity of Our Lord I
Christmas Eve

Lectionary	First Lesson	Psalm	Second Lesson	Gospel
Revised Common	Isa. 9:2-7	Psalm 96	Titus 2:11-14	Luke 2:1-14, (15-20)
Episcopal (BCP)	Isa. 9:2-4, 6-7	Psalm 96 or 96:1-4, 11-12	Titus 2:11-14	Luke 2:1-14, (15-20)
Roman Catholic	Isa. 9:1-6	Ps. 96:1-3, 11-13	Titus 2:11-14	Luke 2:1-14
Lutheran (LBW)	Isa. 9:2-7	Psalm 96	Titus 2:11-14	Luke 2:1-20

FIRST LESSON: ISAIAH 9:2-7

Does this messianic hymn in its current context in Isaiah look forward to an as-yet unrealized time and an as-yet unborn child? Or does it speak from some recognizable moment in Isaiah's experience and refer to a current king? The poetry is not really constructed as an oracle—most of the verbs are present or past tense, and the events described seem already to have transpired. The future glory seems grounded in victorious events of the apparently recent past. Many interpreters think that the piece was probably composed for either Josiah's or Hezekiah's coronation, but (like Psalm 2, for example) it finds a new function here in Isaiah as it looks at "the former time" (Isa. 9:1) and the coming of God's promised Messiah. It presents a traditional picture of a Davidic monarch, as 11:1-9 also does a little later, and describes the day when the Israelite inhabitants of land annexed by Assyria are released from foreign oppression (the "darkness" of 9:2) by royal rescue (the "light").

The "you" of vv. 3-4 seems now to Christian readers to refer to Jesus (or perhaps to God), although it once praised the king who first heard the words at his coronation, and Isaiah likely thinks it addresses the future monarch. This king causes jubilant celebration among the populace (v. 3) because of a military victory that is as great as Gideon's rout of the Midianites in Judges 7:15-25. The battle has been so decisive that there will no longer even be need for an army, since all the soldiers' boots and uniforms are burned in a great celebratory bonfire (v. 5).

When the hymn says "a child has been born to us" and "a son given for us" it calls to mind God's adoption of the king on the day of his coronation in Psalm 2: "You are my son, today I have begotten you" (2:7). Christians who confess Jesus as the Messiah, however, have heard in Isaiah's words instead an interpretation of the infancy stories in Matthew 1–2 and Luke

1–2. Luke himself may have been the first to do so, for his words in Gabriel's annunciation to Mary that Jesus "will be called the Son of the Most High, and the Lord God will give to him the throne of his ancestor David" (Luke 1:32) certainly sound like Isa. 9:6 ("Mighty God") and 9:7 ("endless peace for the throne of David and his kingdom"). In the context of Isaiah, the honorary coronation names "Wonderful Counselor, Mighty God [that is, as strong as God or armed with divine power], Everlasting Father, Prince of Peace" in v. 6 are very similar to names given to Egyptian pharaohs at their accessions, although the second title has obviously taken on deeper meaning to Christians whose confession of Jesus as God's son attributes to him divine identity that was not given even to David in ancient Israel.

In its Christian context, the hymn praises a literal baby rather than a metaphorical one (the adult king adopted as God's son), so the thought that the government should rest on a newborn's shoulders is startling in a way the original may not have been. The wonderful irony is best captured in the words of an old carol:

> This little Babe, so few days old, is come to rifle Satan's fold.
> All hell doth at his presence quake, though he himself for cold do shake.
> Yet in his weak unarmed wise, the gates of hell he will surprise.

SECOND LESSON: TITUS 2:11-14

Titus 2:11-14 and 3:4-7 strike many interpreters as reminiscent of ancient baptismal liturgies, particularly the language of renouncing evil at 2:12 and the "water of rebirth and renewal" at 3:5. Both passages refer to Jesus' "manifestation" (2:13) or "appearance" (3:4) as a revelation of God, and both describe Christians as saved by God's grace (2:11; 3:15) and awaiting hopefully the completion of God's redemption (2:13; 3:7). The lectionary passage follows the detailing of household responsibilities in 2:1-10 and concludes with an endorsement of "Titus's" ecclesiastical authority in v. 15, both of which provide helpful reminders that theological reflections on the nature of Jesus' person and work in the New Testament are seldom merely theoretical, but arise out of the church's embodied experience. In this case, the depiction of Christ in royal or imperial terms functions to underscore what the Pastor (the author of the Pastoral Epistles) thinks is important to preserve about the hierarchical structure of church life.

The passage is a single long sentence in Greek, although most translations divide it for the sake of English style. The main verb is "appeared" and its subject is "the grace of God" (v. 11). Everything else in these three verses describes the consequences of that appearance of God's grace in Jesus Christ. The appearance of grace is specified as *saving* grace for all people. The NRSV helpfully translates the adjective "saving" as a noun, "salvation," but it is important to see that what follows describes God's grace rather than the human race's salvation. The first circumstantial participial phrase begins with *paideuousa*, which is from the verb for "train" and is related to the word for "child" and refers specifically to education or formation. God's grace forms us as we form little children by teaching them, and it is saving grace because it teaches us (1) to "renounce impiety and worldly passions" and (2) to live "self-controlled, upright, and godly" lives (v. 12). The contrast between "before" and "after" is common in early Christian discussions of the results of baptism (cf. Rom. 13:12-13) and is often accompanied by the imagery of changing clothes to signify the change of lifestyle (for instance, Col. 3:9-10).

The second participial phrase modifies "us" rather than grace, but nevertheless directs attention to divine more than to human action. We live, says the Pastor, "while we wait for the blessed hope and manifestation of glory" (v. 13). Although the Pastor exhibits far less urgent expectation of the parousia than Paul does, he knows it is yet an essential component of Christian confession. The difference between the two is that the Pastor's emphasis is on the life people live "in the present age"—we live while we hope—while Paul's emphasis is on our hope of God's glory (Rom. 5:1)—we hope while we live.

As in Paul, so the Pastor says the content of Christian hope is "glory," both the glory of the great God and the glory of our savior Jesus Christ (v. 13). The final phrase of the passage is a relative clause that describes Christ. He gave himself on our behalf in order that he might (1) redeem and (2) cleanse or purify us (v. 14). The result is a people that belongs to him, although *periousion* really says more about the distinctiveness or peculiarity of a possession than about the act of possessing. "A people of his own" recalls biblical language about election in such places as Exod. 19:5-6; Deut. 7:6; 14:2; 32:9. Christ's people are described as "zealous for good deeds," which explains the Pastor's characteristic concern to enumerate the ethical qualities of the redeemed life.

Jouette M. Bassler points out that this brief summary of the consequences of baptism in Titus 2 considers the whole sweep of the Christ event from Christ's "appearance" (v. 11) to his "appearance of glory" (v. 13). The two manifestations, one past in Jesus of Nazareth, and one future in hope and glory, mark the boundaries of God's plan of salvation. Jesus does not "come" in the future, as Christians of more apocalyptic orientations would have it, but is "manifested" as so often the Roman emperors are described as doing ("A Plethora of Epiphanies: Christology in the Pastoral Letters," *Princeton Seminary Bulletin* 17 ns [1996]: 322–23). There is therefore in this text a quite clear, if implicit, contrast between Christ who is the authentic sovereign and the Emperor whose authority is merely derived (3:1; 1 Tim. 2:2; Rom. 13:1).

GOSPEL: LUKE 2:1-20

Luke's account of the census (2:1) is, to put it gently, a bit difficult to understand. We know of some censuses taken during roughly this period of time, but none close enough to account for Mary and Joseph's travel at the time of Jesus' birth. Furthermore, we know of no census taken under these peculiar conditions. Sending all people to their ancestral homes would have been as chaotic an undertaking in antiquity as it would be today, since, among other things, it could hardly provide for immigrants or those with unknown or uncertain heritage. Despite heroic and creative attempts by professional and amateur interpreters alike over the centuries, Luke's report simply cannot be squared with the rest of the historical data we have about Roman procedures in the first century. It is therefore both more homiletically productive and more respectful of the sort of book Luke appears to have written to focus on what Luke thinks it means that world history is the stage on which God acts out the divine plan than it is to wrestle with the historical contradictions present in this particular story. (See Raymond E. Brown, *The Birth of the Messiah* [rev. and exp. ed.; Garden City, N.Y.: Doubleday, 1996] for a discussion of the historical problems.)

Luke knows, as do all early Christians and many non-Christians of the day, that Jesus is from Nazareth of Galilee. Luke also knows, however, that Micah prophesied that the Messiah should be born in Bethlehem (Mic. 5:2), since that is the hometown of David. This story of the census and Jesus' birth in Bethlehem provides Luke, among many other things, with a way to resolve that contradiction. (Matthew and John answer the same difficulty by other means—see below, the story from Matthew 2 for the Second Sunday after Christmas—and Mark appears not to be concerned about the discrepancy at all.) For Luke, it seems, who frequently locates the story of Jesus and the church within the context of wider events on the world stage (compare, for example, the prophetic call of the Baptist in Luke 3:1 or the death of Herod in Acts 12:20-23), salvation history often parallels world history, but it operates according to God's plan on God's terms. In this case, to say that it is the census that takes Mary and Joseph to Bethlehem means that Caesar may think that he is in control, moving human beings around like pieces on a gameboard, but it is God who in fact is the

THE NATIVITY OF OUR LORD I—CHRISTMAS EVE

prime mover in this story. The census, for Luke, functions to explain how Jesus, who was known everywhere to be from Nazareth, should come to be born in Bethlehem, which is where Scripture says he should be born. It is no accident, of course, that Mary should go into labor on this journey, because it is as theologically necessary that the Messiah be born in Bethlehem as it is theologically impossible that a prophet should perish apart from Jerusalem (Luke 13:33). It may also be that Luke envisions the pouring of people into Bethlehem, and the worldwide movement of the entire population under circumstances such as these, to be some kind of foreshadowing of the expectation given voice in Isa. 66:18-23 and elsewhere in early Judaism that in the last days all the nations of earth will converge on Jerusalem to worship the God of Israel (cf. Tobit 13:11).

Mary swaddles her newborn as a loving parent would ("wrapped him in bands of cloth," as the NRSV very helpfully puts it) and lays him in a manger "because there was no place for them in the inn" (2:7). There is no mention of a stable, although popular piety makes an understandable assumption about it: an animal trough (manger) must have been somewhere where animals were kept, perhaps in a stable. Ancient Christian piety decided the manger was instead in a cave, as the second-century *Protevangelium Jacobi* describes it. The fact that Luke mentions the manger three times (2:7, 12, 16) and even calls it a "sign" has invited speculation since ancient times. Brown thinks it likely that the image is designed to reverse the one in Isa. 1:3: "The ox knows its owner, and the donkey its master's crib; but Israel does not know, my people do not understand." The fact that the shepherds honor the king Jesus in a manger may mean, says Brown, that "God's people have begun to know the manger of their Lord" (*Birth of the Messiah*, 419).

The shepherds in the field (2:8) are witnesses, of course, both to the angelic visitation (2:9-14) and to the baby himself (2:16), but they are also reminders to the reader of Luke's Gospel that shepherds are *supposed* to be in "the city of David" (2:11) where the great shepherd himself watched his father's flocks before being summoned by Samuel and anointed king (1 Sam. 16:11-13). The shepherds who visit the baby Jesus may in fact represent the great unwashed masses of Jews who were unable to maintain much religious scrupulosity on account of their work and were widely suspected of dishonesty, and they may therefore prefigure the other marginal and despised people with whom the adult Jesus surrounds himself during his ministry, but if they do, Luke gives little indication that he thinks so.

The angel announces "good news [that is, the *gospel*] of great joy for all the people" (2:10) in words that are designed to remind one both of imperial proclamations ("this day" and "peace among those whom he favors") and of Isa. 9:6-7 ("For a child has been born for us, a son given to us" and "there shall be endless peace for the throne of David and his kingdom"). Instead of calling the child "Wonderful Counselor" or "Prince of Peace" in Isaiah's words, though, the angel calls Jesus "Savior," "Christ," and "Lord," which are for him standard titles of Christian faith.

The angel's "sign" of the manger (2:12) is fulfilled in the shepherds' discovery of the family, just as Gabriel's prophecy about Jesus' name (1:31) is fulfilled at the Temple when Jesus is circumcised (2:21). Although Luke does not explicitly mention the meaning of the name Jesus (in Hebrew, Joshua) as Matthew does (Matt. 1:21), the notion that "Yahweh saves" is surely implicit in the naming of the child born to be the "savior" (Luke 2:11). Heavenly messengers and intermediaries like these angels populate many of Luke's stories in both volumes of his work, and their function is to assure the reader that God is moving the story forward, despite the sometimes puzzling movements of apparently strong human characters in the narrative.

The shepherds go "with haste" to see what the angels have told them about (2:16) just as Mary earlier went with haste to see Elizabeth (1:39). Salvation is literally breaking into human experience; the speed with which God is acting makes haste the appropriate human response. Unlike the magi in Matthew or the unborn John in Luke 1:41, the shepherds do not worship or greet the infant Jesus, they confirm the truth of the angelic annunciation by finding Mary, Joseph, and the baby just as they have been told. Their response is to "make known" (2:17) the word that the Lord has "made known" to them (2:15), evoking astonishment from their listeners (2:18) and to give glory and praise to God themselves (2:20).

For her part, Mary "ponders" the events in her heart (2:19), much as she will later "treasure" in her heart the intervening events of Jesus' childhood and youth (2:51). The two words share a common root, the verb "to keep," and suggest some ambivalence in Mary's responses to the events of Jesus' birth and childhood and adolescence. Those around her sing and are amazed and rejoice, but Mary keeps these things in her heart. Beverly Roberts Gaventa suggests that the two moments prepare for the two equally ambiguous other mentions of Mary in Luke: at 8:19-21 where it is not clear whether she is distinguished from or included among Jesus' disciples, and at 11:27-28 where Jesus' response to an anonymous woman's exuberant blessing of his (absent) mother is to bless instead those who hear and obey God's word. Does he or does he not include among them the woman who bore him and nursed him? Luke does not say. Only at Acts 1:14, where Mary is among the disciples gathered in the upper room for the selection of Judas's successor among the Twelve do we learn unambiguously that Jesus' mother remains the disciple Luke portrays her as being at the annunciation.

For all that Mary's initial faithful response to Gabriel identifies her as a disciple in Luke's eyes, the ambiguities of the other roles she plays in his two-volume work seem also to reflect the complexities of discipleship. Simeon will later warn her that, because of her remarkable son, "a sword will pierce [her] own soul too" (2:35). It may be that Mary's Christmas pondering is Luke's way of introducing early on, in the midst of angelic joy and human excitement, a hint of the somber reality to come. It is, after all, "necessary" that the Messiah suffer (Luke 24:26). Perhaps we too ought to ponder the implications of welcoming the Messiah's birth, including particularly the necessity of his—and our—suffering, since "no one who puts a hand to the plow and looks back is fit for the kingdom of God" (Luke 9:62).

The Nativity of Our Lord 2
Christmas Day

Lectionary	First Lesson	Psalm	Second Lesson	Gospel
Revised Common	Isa. 52:7-10	Psalm 98	Heb. 1:1-4, (5-12)	John 1:1-14
Episcopal (BCP)	Isa. 52:7-10	Psalm 98 or 98:1-6	Heb. 1:1-12	John 1:1-14
Roman Catholic	Isa. 52:7-10	Ps. 98:1-6	Heb. 1:1-6	John 1:1-18 or 1:1-5, 9-14
Lutheran (LBW)	Isa. 52:7-10	Psalm 97	Heb. 1:1-9	John 1:1-14

FIRST LESSON: ISAIAH 52:7-10

The wider context of this passage is 51:9—52:12, which resembles some psalms of lament that call on God to redress the people's suffering (Psalms 44 and 74; cf. Isa. 63:7—64:12; see the very perceptive argument of Richard J. Clifford, "Isaiah 40–66," in *Harper's Bible Commentary* [ed. James L. Mays; San Francisco: Harper & Row, 1988], 582). That larger context of the lament is itself surrounded by the third and fourth of the Servant Songs (50:4-11 and 52:13—53:12), and this in itself is an important interpretive factor to bear in mind. The announcement on Christmas Day that God has in fact entered human affairs in the birth of Jesus to redeem and restore ruined cities and wounded hearts stands in painful tension with the message broadcast throughout North America in the weeks preceding this day. Instead of celebrating the acquisition of goods by means of our economic power, the preacher is called to name the poverty that surrounds us, the exile, the suffering. The messenger of peace, good news, salvation, and the reign of God speaks not to the satisfied but to the hungry, not to the victorious but to the defeated. Seldom is it so difficult in the church to name and point to that brokenness than on Christmas Day, when we—with the culture—might prefer to congratulate ourselves with a hearty "God bless us every one!"

The segment of the lament that is the lectionary reading follows immediately a description of God's vow to vindicate the divine name and integrity by rescuing the people (Isa. 52:5-6). The lament over Jerusalem's defeat is here answered by the proclamation of God's victory, and opens with a conversation between the sentries whose job is to watch at the city walls. The sentries recognize the approach of the advance team that is bringing word of the army's victory and they exclaim at the beauty of the sight of these "messengers of peace." This peace is not merely the end of a

THE NATIVITY OF OUR LORD 2—CHRISTMAS DAY 47

bloody battle but the very "salvation" of the nation because it demonstrates conclusively that "your God reigns" (v. 7). When it is God who guides and directs the holy warriors, the victory belongs not to the army alone. Moreover, Israel's defeat of its enemies is once again evidence that Yahweh is more powerful than the gods of the nations.

Following the heralds the LORD marches in the victory procession, and the sentries break into song as they report the news (vv. 8-9). They recount God's mighty deeds ("bared his holy arm," v. 10) and imagine, in language reminiscent of Isa. 40:5, that now the whole earth and not only Israel will bear witness to the greatness of God's redemption (v. 10).

Because the church has read a reference to Jesus as Lord in this Isaianic poem that sees "the return of the LORD to Zion" (v. 8), it has long been associated with the nativity. Quotations of or allusions to Isa. 52:7-10 are numerous in the New Testament—in Jesus' "preaching peace" (Acts 10:36; Eph. 2:17) or the church's similar proclamation of peace (Rom. 10:15; Ephesians 2:15-17)—but it is Luke who causes us to think of the baby Jesus when we hear Isaiah's words. At Luke 2:25 the aged Simeon is described as one who "looks for the consolation of Israel" as the sentries in Isaiah 52 do, and the word about the Messiah's birth and presentation in the temple goes out to "all who were looking for the redemption of Israel" (Luke 2:38).

SECOND LESSON: HEBREWS 1:1-9 (-12)

The anonymous author of this extended sermon we call Hebrews opens his book with the solemn affirmation that God has spoken by the prophets "in many and various ways" over time. This gives voice to a profound respect for Jewish tradition, despite the fact that the author will quickly show that the tradition has been left behind in many and various ways because of the advent of God's Son, Jesus. Hebrews is a complex and subtle reflection on a number of bipolar relationships: between God's past and God's future, between tradition and experience, between heaven and earth, and between Christianity and Judaism. While much is rightly made of the author's philosophical sophistication and the function of his Neoplatonic distinction between "shadow" and "reality" (see above, the second lesson from Hebrews 10 on the Fourth Sunday in Advent), it is important to remember that his primary tool is the Bible. Hebrews contains more sustained interpretation of Scripture than does any other New Testament book, and that becomes clear from the first verse.

Neither 1:9 nor 1:12 makes a very logical stopping place for the reading, despite the lectionary's boundaries. The interpreter should either read all the way to v. 14 in order to hold together the entire thought unit or stop with v. 4, since vv. 1-4 constitute the *exordium*, the opening statement of the epistle's primary themes. Even if the liturgical reading stops at v. 9, which accents the joy of Christmas day, or v. 12, which stresses Jesus' endless reign and unchanging glory, the interpretation ought to take account of the author's complete thought. The two uses of Ps. 110:1 at Heb. 1:3 ("he sat down at the right hand of the Majesty on high") and 1:13 ("Sit at my right hand until I make your enemies a footstool for your feet") hold the passage together.

The exegesis of verses from Psalms 2, 104, 45, 102, 110; 2 Samuel 7; and Deuteronomy 32 stands together in vv. 5-13 to interpret the affirmation in 1:4 that Jesus is superior to God's angels because he is God's son. The catena, or chain, of verses is introduced with an allusion to Ps. 110:1, which may just be the most popular Bible verse (meaning, of course, from the Old Testament) in all of early Christianity. Quotations of the verse or allusions to the picture of Jesus sitting at God's right hand are ubiquitous in Christian literature of the first two centuries—from Paul's letters (Rom. 8:34; 1 Cor. 15:25) and the Pauline school (Eph. 1:20; Col. 3:1), to the Gospels (Matt. 22:44; 26:64; Mark 12:36; 14:62; Luke 20:42-43; 22:69), Acts (2:34-35; 5:31; 7:55-56), and Revelation (3:21) to numerous nonbiblical texts—but it is in Hebrews that the Psalm receives its most sustained interpretation. The author quotes or alludes to Ps. 110:1 not only here in the opening verses, but also at 8:1 and 10:12-13. And in 5:6, 10; 6:20; and 7:1-28 he makes use of 110:4: "You are a priest forever, according to the order of Melchizedek."

The reason Psalm 110 is such an enormously popular Scripture text for early Christians is that it helps them to explain where the risen Christ is in relation both to the church and to God. It also helped people in the first decades of the church to balance theologically the increasingly divine status they attributed to Jesus with their continuing devotion to Jewish monotheism. From very soon after the first Easter, but long before the major christological formulations of the fourth and fifth centuries, Christians encountered resistance from their Jewish families and friends who perceived them to be worshiping someone other than the one God of Israel. David M. Hay describes the usefulness of Ps. 110:1 to the first Christian theologians: "Over against expressions like 'Jesus is Lord,' this image [of Jesus at God's right hand] intrinsically affirmed a continuing relationship between the exalted Christ and God, precluding any possibility of conceiving Christ as a new deity dethroning an older one" (*Glory at the Right Hand: Psalm 110 in Early Christianity* [SBLMS 18; Chico, Calif.: Scholars Press, 1973]: 159–60).

One who sits at the right hand of a king—in this case, of God—shares the privileges and prestige of the king. But Hebrews says Jesus is more than a privileged person in God's court, he is God's very Son, which means he is God's heir and co-creator (v. 2), the reflection of God's glory and "the exact imprint of God's very being" (v. 3). This is far greater a likeness than the genetic markers that relate human beings to our parents and our children. For Hebrews, Jesus is the indelible mark left by God's action in the world, by God's very self in relationship to the world. The word that the NRSV renders "imprint" or the NEB "stamp" is *charakter*, the word we took into English as "character." It is used of the mark made on a minted coin or the image left by pressing a signet ring into hot wax, and thus denotes the full authority of the one minting the money or sealing the document. It guarantees the authenticity of a written message as not even a signature does. So for Hebrews, Jesus makes God present in an unprecedented way, even though God's "many and various" words in the past were themselves reflections of God's will.

GOSPEL: JOHN 1:1-14 (-18)

The prologue to the Fourth Gospel really extends to v. 18, and the Christmas affirmation of Jesus' enfleshedness is most explicit in 14-18, so it seems best to treat the poem in its entirety. Its hymnic character and only loose relation to the rest of John (the primary image of Jesus as the Word, for example, never occurs again) have suggested to most interpreters that the passage had a life prior to its inclusion at the beginning of John. The original hymn has itself apparently been interpreted—perhaps by the later editor of the Gospel—with additional lines. God's children are described in v. 12a as those who have "accepted" the Word, and that acceptance is itself interpreted in v. 12b as "believing in his name." The notion is further elaborated in 12c-13 by an apposition between human and divine begetting. So also, after the second and fourth strophes of the hymn, someone has inserted into the poem parenthetical prose descriptions of John's preaching and ministry (vv. 6-9, 15). Raymond E. Brown suggests the original shape of the poem looked something like this, before its appropriation and interpretation in the Fourth Gospel (*The Gospel According to John I–XII* [AB 29; Garden City, N. Y.: Doubleday, 1966], 3–4):

> [1] In the beginning was the Word,
> and the Word was in God's presence,
> and the Word was God.
>
> [2] He was present with God in the beginning.

> ³ Through him all things came into being,
> and apart from him not a thing came to be.
> ⁴ That which had come to be in him was life,
> and this life was the light of [human beings].
> ⁵ The light shines on in the darkness,
> for the darkness did not overcome it.
>
> ¹⁰ He was in the world,
> and the world was made by him;
> yet the world did not recognize him.
> ¹¹ To his own he came;
> yet his own people did not accept him.
> ¹² But all those who did accept him
> he empowered to become God's children.
>
> ¹⁴ And the Word became flesh
> and made his dwelling among us,
> And we have seen his glory,
> the glory of an only Son coming from the Father,
> filled with enduring love.
> ¹⁶ And of his fullness
> we have all had a share—
> love in place of love.

The initial words "in the beginning" naturally call the first words of Genesis to mind, when God speaks the universe into being. The early hymnwriter or even the Fourth Evangelist himself seems to think here of Jesus' being at God's side at that moment, even acting with God or on God's behalf to create the ordered world out of chaos. Much the same thing has long been said of God's wisdom, as Prov. 8:22-31 does:

> The LORD created me at the beginning of his work,
>   the first of his acts of long ago.
> Ages ago I was set up,
>   at the first, before the beginning of the earth.
> When there were no depths I was brought forth,
>   when there were no springs abounding with water.
> Before the mountains had been shaped,
>   before the hills, I was brought forth—
> when he had not yet made earth and fields,
>   or the world's first bits of soil.
> When he established the heavens, I was there,
>   when he drew a circle on the face of the deep,

when he made firm the skies above,
> when he established the fountains of the deep,
when he assigned to the sea its limit,
> so that the waters might not transgress his command,
when he marked out the foundations of the earth,
> then I was beside him, like a master worker;
and I was daily his delight,
> rejoicing before him always,
rejoicing in his inhabited world
> and delighting in the human race.

This image of personified Wisdom as God's co-creator in Proverbs 8 is also reflected in Sir. 24:3, where Wisdom says of herself, "I came forth from the mouth of the Most High, and covered the earth like a mist" (see below, the Second Sunday after Christmas). The Wisdom of Solomon similarly equates God's word and wisdom: "O God of my ancestors and LORD of mercy, who have made all things by your word, and by your wisdom have formed humankind" (Wisd. 9:1-2). This has suggested to a number of interpreters that the christological hymn that begins the Fourth Gospel implicitly describes Jesus as the incarnation of God's wisdom. Since Jews of the first century often say of God's wisdom what their Stoic neighbors say of divine reason (which they call *logos* or "word"), that it holds the universe together, orders life, and makes the divine accessible to human beings, there is good reason to think not only of God's creative word but also God's creative wisdom as the conceptual context within which the Johannine prologue reflects on the incarnation.

First Sunday after Christmas

Lectionary	First Lesson	Psalm	Second Lesson	Gospel
Revised Common	1 Sam. 2:18-20, 26	Psalm 148	Col. 3:12-17	Luke 2:41-52
Episcopal (BCP)	Isa. 61:10—62:3	Psalm 147 or 147:13-21	Gal. 3:23-25; 4:4-7	John 1:1-18
Roman Catholic	1 Sam. 1:20-22, 24-28	Ps. 128:1-5	1 John 3:1-2, 21-24	Luke 2:41-52
Lutheran (LBW)	Jer. 31:10-13	Psalm 111	Heb. 2:10-18	Luke 2:41-52

FIRST LESSON: JEREMIAH 31:10-13; 1 SAMUEL 1:20-22, 24-28; ISAIAH 61:10—62:3; 1 SAMUEL 2:18-20, 26

The various lectionaries make widely differing choices about the Old Testament and epistle texts for the First Sunday after Christmas.

Jeremiah 31:10-13. The oracle from which this passage is taken begins at v. 7 extends to v. 14. It describes the return of Israel from exile as the people's lamentation turns to rejoicing and their grief to thanksgiving. God is here both a parent ("a father to Israel," v. 9) and a king ("will keep them as a shepherd a flock," v. 10). Israel is both God's firstborn child and the nation wisely led by a caring monarch. Verses 12-14 describe the homecoming party: singing and good food and wine, dancing in the streets, and lavish cultic celebrations, not a bad description of some Christmas festivities.

1 Samuel 1:20-22, 24-28. The first of the two possible texts from 1 Samuel tells the story of Hannah's conception of Samuel and her dedication of him to the Lord as a nazirite. The laws pertaining to these Israelites who are "consecrated" to God are listed in Num. 6:1-21, and the other most well-known of nazirites is Samson, whose story is remarkably similar to Samuel's (Judges 13). Both men are born to devoted but barren mothers, and while Hannah herself makes the decision to dedicate her baby to God, Manoah and his wife receive divine instruction to do the same for Samson (Judges 13:5).

In the story of Samuel, God's overcoming of Hannah's barrenness both reflects stories about other remarkable births (particularly Samson's, but also Isaac's) and also becomes a model for later ones. Luke, in particular, is greatly taken with the story of Hannah and Elkanah and Samuel. Both John's and Jesus' birth and infancy stories are shaped by it, and Mary's song of praise in Luke 1:46-55 is clearly modeled after Hannah's in 1 Sam. 2:1-10. It is particularly the portrait of Hannah as one who trusts God that shows in Luke's picture of Mary, since it is Hannah alone who knows that she has prayed for a child and has promised to dedicate him to God. The lectionary's deletion of v. 23 from the story is a bit odd, since that sentence only reinforces the story's emphasis on Hannah's faith in God and portrays Elkanah as not quite understanding what is going on—yet another detail that seems to have influenced Luke's description of Zechariah.

Isaiah 61:10—62:3. The assigned reading is a combination of two separate passages: the song of thanksgiving that concludes the poem of 61:1-11 and the prayer that begins 62:1-12. The song of thanksgiving pictures God dressing the people of Jerusalem in the clothing of "salvation" and "righteousness" in the joyful way that a bride and groom dress for their wedding (v. 10). The image then shifts to an agricultural one, and God's vindication of the people is compared to a blooming garden that comes to life in the spring (v. 11; cf. Jer. 31:12 where the same metaphor is used). The flowering of God's restored people will be "before all the nations," a reminder that redemption is as much a vindication of God's honor and integrity as it is of the nation's own interests. Christian preaching in the modern age has become increasingly anthropocentric, concentrating its attention on humanity's need for salvation more than on God's righteous salvation. God redeems the creation and restores the people's justice for God's sake, because the creation belongs to God in the first place and because the demonstration of righteousness "before all the nations" manifests God's character to the world.

The words of the prayer in Isa. 62:1-3 likewise portray God's vindication of Zion as shining like the sun or a torch (v. 1) that captures the attention of all peoples and elicits from even their monarchs divine worship (v. 2). The rescued city is now not only reborn as a garden after the winter is past (cf. 61:11) but also a bride whose status and name change at her marriage. The specific new names that God gives to Jerusalem—"My Delight Is in Her" and "Married"—are not articulated until v. 4, but the metaphor of name-change begins in v. 2. There is here in Third Isaiah a conviction that is later central to Christian writers like Paul who also speak of God's grace as transformation. Rather than offering only to forget the past or to wipe clean the slate, as if divine grace were merely amnesty, God invariably changes those who are redeemed. As Paul describes it in Romans, God justifies the ungodly before they even know their sinful plight and at the very point where they are least powerless in the face of it. God's acquittal of the guilty, however, makes just the unjust by handing the justified over to the lordship of righteousness and enabling them to "become obedient from the heart" (Rom. 6:17).

1 Samuel 2:18-20, 26. The second reading from 1 Samuel looks at the next stage of Samuel's life, after his mother has kept her vow to dedicate him and he has been installed in the Temple service. The boy Samuel is contrasted with "the sons of Eli [who] were scoundrels" (2:12). Although we do not learn Hophni and Phinehas's names until v. 34, their appalling abuse of the sacrificial system and extortion of their neighbors are held up by the narrator for scorn: "they treated the offerings of the LORD with contempt" (v. 17). How different is young Samuel, who is humble (he wears only simple priestly dress) and who is favored by both God and the people (v. 26).

The elderly Eli approaches death apparently worried that his badly behaved sons will be poor successors to him and he attempts to get them to mend their ways, but they are unrepentant and the narrator explains that God has already sealed their fate (v. 25). The language of v. 26, that "the boy Samuel continued to grow both in stature and in favor with the LORD and with the people" is used and adapted by Luke to describe the boy Jesus in Luke 2:40 ("the child grew and became strong, filled with wisdom; and the favor of God was upon him") and the young John ("the child grew and became strong in spirit," 1:80), just as Hannah herself has served as a model for Mary in Luke's infancy narrative.

SECOND LESSON: HEBREWS 2:10-18; 1 JOHN 3:1-2, 21-24; GALATIANS 3:23-25; 4:4-7; COLOSSIANS 3:12-17

Once again the various lectionaries diverge widely in their choices of epistle lesson, but all four share a focus on believers' status as children of God.

Hebrews 2:10-18. The notion of incarnation assists the author of Hebrews to make two parallel christological claims: Jesus is both able to atone for us as one of us, and is also able to help us when we are tested. It is a matter first of *ontology*, of standing with us on the necessary side of the human-divine relationship so as to make appropriate and effective sacrifice on our behalf. But it is also a matter of *empathy*, of Jesus' capacity to understand our experience because he has shared it.

The thought begins in the beginning of chapter 2 where interpretation of Ps. 8:4-6 helps the author to set up Jesus' status as the salvation "pioneer" (v. 10). In Hebrew, the psalmist marvels that God has granted humanity such exalted status in the world, making people only "a little lower than

God" (Ps. 8:5). In a Greek translation, however, the words of the Psalm become susceptible of another, very different reading, which the writer of Hebrews clearly considers the correct one. The word for "humanity" in Hebrew can be rendered with a word that means the same thing in Greek but is frequently also used to denote a single (male) human being. This interpretation becomes even more possible when the parallel clause in the Hebrew poetry ("mortals" in the NRSV) can be translated "son of man." Since the latter (in Greek) becomes a technical title for Jesus (that is, *the* "Son of Man") in many Christian vocabularies, it is quite understandable that the writer of Hebrews should find Jesus in Psalm 8.

The second interpretive move in the exegesis of the Psalm (again in Greek rather than in Hebrew) recognizes the two meanings possible in the adverb *brachu* in Ps. 8:5. The text either says that God made Jesus "a little bit" lower than the angels or "for a little while" lower than the angels. The distinction concerns whether the adverb is taken spatially or temporally. The Hebrew original is most assuredly spatial in orientation. Human beings are obviously lower on the scale of divinity than angels. In Hebrews, though, Jesus is not a bit lower than God, except for that period of time when he descends to earth to carry out his high priestly function and then return to God. Jesus' sharing our human life "for a little while" is sufficient to establish our connection with him such that he will take us with him to heaven. Jesus provides the link between heaven and earth. He is thus the pioneer of salvation who leads those who follow in the expedition that is traveling to heaven.

In the very same sentence that identifies Jesus as the leader (v. 10), though, the metaphor shifts from an expedition to a family. Jesus the pioneer is also the first of the many brothers and sisters who are God's children. Because he is one of them, Jesus can tell the children about their common parent (as Ps. 22:22 says he does; Heb. 2:11) and assist them as an older sibling does when they are tempted (2:18). The family language in Hebrews, as throughout the New Testament, reflects both the social context of early Christianity (the people met in homes) and theological affirmations about who God is and how we are related to God through Jesus. This is structurally akin to the Pauline baptismal affirmation that God is *Abba* (cf. the discussion of Galatians 3–4 below).

1 John 3:1-2, 21-24. The thought unit within which 3:1-2 is found begins at 2:28 and continues through 3:3. Becoming children of God is a function of God's love, says the Elder. This could be a perceptive glimpse into the obvious were it not likely the affirmation reflects a serious—and recent—breach within the Christian community from which and to which the Elder writes. Who could imagine Christians hating one another or refusing to take care of one another as the Elder suggests in 3:11-17? What is at stake here is not merely the kind of callous but distorted piety described in James 2:15-16 ("If a brother or sister is naked and lacks daily food, and one of you says to them, 'Go in peace; keep warm and eat your fill,' and yet you do not supply their bodily needs, what is the good of that?"). In 1 John we see instead a Christian community that has divided over its interpretation of its own tradition and each part has essentially excommunicated the other (see Raymond E. Brown's reconstruction of Johannine history, *The Community of the Beloved Disciple: The Life, Loves, and Hates of an Individual Church in New Testament Times* [New York: Paulist, 1979]).

Those who are not in the Elder's community, he says, "went out from us, but they did not belong to us; for if they had belonged to us, they would have remained with us. But by going out they made it plain that none of them belongs to us" (1 John 2:19). The schism is described as the departure of the secessionists. They are the ones who say they have fellowship with God but, according to the Elder, walk in darkness (1:6), who deceive themselves by saying they have no sin (1:8). They too believe they are God's children (3:1), but they apparently believe they have achieved the ultimate form of that intimate relationship with God, since the Elder contrasts them with his own flock who know they are God's children but do not yet know what they will be at the last day. This sounds a bit as though the Elder seeks to trump the secessionists' exalted view of their status, since he assures his own group that they are now God's children, but they can look forward to even greater status: they will be like God at the eschaton because they will "see him as he is" (3:2). This reintroduces some traditional apocalyptic notions into a community whose faith has previously been shaped and nurtured by the Fourth Gospel's greatly reduced expectations of the end. In John, everyone who believes in Jesus has already passed from death to life (John 5:24), and that seems to be just what the secessionists say about themselves. In this later generation of Johannine Christianity, though, such realized eschatology no longer seems to comfort the Elder as it once did the persecuted community for whom the Gospel was written, but instead cultivates religious narcissism, ethical passivity, and disregard for brothers and sisters. To correct such distortions, he reminds his remnant congregation that God has not finished with them yet and their identity as God's children awaits its final fulfillment ("what we will be has not yet been revealed," 3:2).

The second part of the lectionary passage, 3:21-24, is also part of a larger thought unit, 3:18-24. What it means to have one's heart condemn oneself (v. 21) is clearly a function of guilt incurred through sin, but it may

FIRST SUNDAY AFTER CHRISTMAS

also have to do with anxiety about one's place in the world. The question may have arisen among the Elder's little band that the secessionists were perhaps right and they wrong. The concrete need to "know that we are from the truth and . . . reassure our hearts" (3:19) may stem from the community's comparing of itself to the secessionists, since the latter appear to be more successful ("the world listens to them," 4:5) and may even be economically wealthier (whoever "has the world's goods," 3:17). The Elder's flock can be comforted in the face of such doubts because there exist objective measures that they are "from the truth." If they love one another "not in word or speech, but in truth and action" (3:18), if they obey God's commandments to believe in Jesus and to love one another (3:23), they have no need to fear.

Galatians 3:23-25; 4:4-7. The two pieces of the designated reading, Gal. 3:23-25 and 4:4-7, make an odd combination, since the first part comes from one part of the larger argument (3:19-25) and the second part from another (3:26—4:7). Galatians 3:25, the termination of the first half, even ends midsentence. The result is something of a *Reader's Digest* version of Paul's argument. If the truncated text is read aloud in worship, the preacher will do well to read the entire pericope in the study.

The immediate context begins at 3:19. Paul has argued that the Galatians are justified and experience the Spirit of God as a consequence of their trusting the good news of Christ's death and resurrection rather than their having obeyed God's law (3:1-5). The biblical basis for this argument is Gen. 15:6, which says God counted Abraham's faith as righteousness, so all who similarly trust God are Abraham's descendants. Moses received the law 430 years after God's covenant-making with Abraham, so the law can scarcely annul the terms of that prior relationship (3:15-18). The law is therefore a blind alley in people's search for a right relationship with God, since the way of faith has been established previously on the basis of trust.

At 3:19, then, Paul asks the logical question, "Why then the law?" If God's promise to Abraham is what assures Gentile Christians of their membership in God's family, and if the law could never grant the life it apparently offered, then why did God give the law at all? The answer: because of transgressions. The law was a temporary measure, designed to keep people from grabbing at the promise of God on their own before Jesus, its intended recipient (note Paul's emphasis on the singular "descendent" in v. 16), arrived to accept it and to share it with all who trust his faithful obedience to God (3:22). The law functioned until the time Christ came as a "disciplinarian," as the NRSV puts it, a household slave who watches children to see that they stay out of trouble until they are old enough to inherit the responsibilities and privileges to which they are entitled. With Christ, Paul says, whose absolute trust in God and faithful obedience to God's will were demonstrated in his death on the cross, believers share the promise God made to Abraham.

The creation of the church by Jesus through baptism into him (3:27-28) establishes family relationships among believers. The thought unit, 4:1-7, attends to the transformation of slaves into children and therefore heirs at baptism. Even children born to a family are "no better than slaves," which means they have no rights with regard to their inheritance "until the date set by the father" (v. 2). This means for Paul that the Christ-event is not a capricious or desperate act of God, forced by the failures of previous attempts to effect righteousness, but has been planned for in God's will (or testament or covenant) from the start. It is the fullness of God's time that brings Jesus' birth "of a woman" (v. 4). God sends the Son to be not just any child, either, but a Jewish child, "born under the law," as are we all, whether Jewish or Gentile (v. 5). Only by becoming a curse for those who are cursed (cf. 3:10-14) does Christ make us by adoption to be children of God with full rights of inheritance (4:5, 7).

The *Abba* language for God at v. 6 (see also Rom. 8:14-17; Mark 14:36) probably does not suggest any greater intimacy than any other word for "father," as has so often been alleged. The word likely stays in Aramaic for Greek-speaking Christians at worship because liturgical language is inherently slow to change. North Americans, for example, still frequently use sixteenth-century Elizabethan language in the Lord's Prayer even at the end of the twentieth century, although we do so less often these days in other prayers. Early Christianity is rife with other examples of liturgical vocabulary in Hebrew (*amen, halleluia*) or Aramaic (*marana tha*) on the lips of Greek speakers. Foreign languages seem to carry an aura of holiness about them (cf. the quasi-magical sound to Jesus' Aramaic words in Mark 5:42). We do not have to be first-century people to get a feel for that. Although we might translate *Abba* as "father," perhaps when we are wrestling mightily in the church with the impact of using gender-specific language about God, to keep God's parental name in another language allows us to talk about our shared experience of adoption without pressing the issue of gender.

Colossians 3:12-17. The baptismal language ("clothe yourselves," Col. 3:12) describes the new life in Christ in corporate rather than individual terms. The personal anxiety that is evoked by the religious worldview propounded by the outsiders (some of whose religious positions can be inferred from Col. 2:18-23) could make for a tremendous sense of competition among members of the community to whom this letter is addressed. Perhaps they think, "If it is my responsibility to take care of my own soul and to assure its proper access to God by means of these many religious behaviors and appropriate doctrine, then I have no need or desire to care about anyone else." The author's emphasis on harmony (v. 14) and evocation of Paul's "body" language to describe the church (v. 15), particularly in the context of worship (v. 16), tweaks the noses of the opponents whose complicated prescriptions for right worship have heretofore terrorized the congregation. Religious terrorism (whether about ethics or piety or doctrine) withers in the face of the author's repeated emphasis on thanksgiving for the preemptive love of God that transfers believers from death to life.

Compassion, kindness, humility, meekness, and patience (3:12) are virtues familiar from other lists in Christian, pagan, and Jewish moral exhortation, but they take on specific content here when the author uses Christ as the model for them. To "bear with one another" (v. 13) recalls Paul's invitation to "bear one another's burdens and so fulfill the law of Christ" (Gal. 6:2), and to forgive as the Lord has forgiven echoes the petition of the Lord's Prayer, "forgive us . . . as we forgive" (Matt. 6:12; Luke 11:4). All these virtues in Colossians 3 are held together by love, which the author says "binds everything together in perfect harmony" (Col. 3:14).

The "peace of Christ" should rule in the hearts of believers (3:15), which acknowledges that ethics in the Christian community cannot easily be reduced to rules or personal virtues. The word for "rule" is a sports image, referring to the umpire in the public games who sets the boundaries of the playing field and calls various moves "safe" or "out." The peace of Christ, or the reconciliation between God and sinners established by Christ's death, functions in the church to bind believers together "in the one body" (v. 15; cf. 1 Cor. 12:12-27; Rom. 12:4-5).

The final exhortations concern corporate worship, as contrasted with the private worship apparently envisioned by the opponents who call for the worship of (or perhaps with) angels (2:18). This is a call for the church to be the church, since its very life is the worship of God. For the author of Colossians, it is constituted by teaching and encouragement with the gospel ("the word of Christ"), singing "psalms, hymns, and spiritual songs" (v. 16), and giving thanks to God through Jesus Christ, in whose name or for whose sake or under whose authority all of life is lived.

GOSPEL: LUKE 2:41-52; JOHN 1:1-18

Luke opens and closes his initial narrative in Jerusalem in the temple of God. The first scene shows Zechariah the priest at his temple service (Luke

1:5-23); this final scene has the boy Jesus again in the temple (2:41-52). The great middle section of the Gospel will take place away from the holy city, largely in Galilee (3:1—9:50), and on the long journey back to Jerusalem (9:51—19:28) where the climactic story of Jesus' crucifixion and resurrection will also take place (cf. 24:53). Acts opens as well in Jerusalem, but moves out from there, at Jesus' command and in the power of the Holy Spirit, to Judea and Samaria "and to the ends of the earth" (Acts 1:8). Geography carries symbolic significance for Luke; revelation really ought to take place in the holy city.

At the age of twelve, the traditional age of a boy's study of the law, Jesus accompanies his parents and other relatives to Jerusalem for the Passover celebration (Luke 2:41). Luke says the trip is habitual for the family ("as usual"), which marks them as conventionally devout Jews, an impression later reinforced by the rest of Luke's story. Jesus goes to the synagogue in Nazareth "as [is] his custom" (4:16), and Luke frequently adds to Mark's stories evidence of Jesus' piety, such as prayer (for instance, at his baptism in 3:21) and compassion (for instance, his healing of the slave's ear in 22:51). This is essential to Luke's Christology, contributing as it does to this picture of Jesus as an "innocent" man who will be unjustly martyred (23:47).

The pious adolescent makes a pilgrimage with the apparent purpose of studying with learned men, but he teaches rather than learns. Although he asks questions (v. 46), it is Jesus' own answers that astound the teachers (v. 47). He is more than pious; he is precocious, and Luke's mention of "all who heard him" (v. 47) suggests that maybe the religious prodigy has drawn something of a crowd. The bystanders are amazed and Mary and Joseph are astonished (v. 48), although the reader of the Gospel must surely wonder why Mary, at least, is surprised at Jesus' performance after what the angel Gabriel told her before he was born (1:30-35) and what the shepherds presumably said to her about their visit on the night of his birth (2:15-20).

Jesus tells his parents it is "necessary" that he be in his Father's house (2:49). Alternative translations are that he must be "among my Father's people" or "involved in my Father's affairs" (which was the choice behind the KJV's "about my Father's business"), but the meanings are not materially different, in light of Luke's obvious fondness for the temple as God's house and the physical manifestation of God's faithful presence among the people. Whether Jesus speaks of God's house or people or business, it is *necessary* that he be part of it. This is the first of some twenty-eight times in Luke-Acts that the divine necessity of Jesus' life and death appear as evidence of God's plan to save the world (Luke 4:43; 9:22; 13:33; 24:46;

Acts 3:20-21, to choose only a few examples). Although the boy seems, as other precocious children have, to be somewhat self-absorbed and therefore careless about needlessly worrying his parents (a trait that might have detracted from his image as a model religious figure), Luke says instead that Jesus acts under divine compulsion. It is necessary for God that Jesus be in his Father's house with his Father's people and doing his Father's work.

The poignancy of the parent-child relationship, even when the child is the Son of the Most High, is present in Mary's question to Jesus, "Child, why have you treated us like this? Look, your father and I have been searching for you in great anxiety" (2:48) and is coupled with Mary and Joseph's misunderstanding (v. 50) about Jesus' identity and mission. All of this reinforces the impression of ambivalence we get from Mary's "pondering" the events of Jesus' birth and her "treasuring" the mixed blessings of his remarkable childhood (v. 51).

(For John 1:1-18, see the Gospel for The Nativity of Our Lord 2— Christmas Day.)

The Name of Jesus (January 1)

Lectionary	First Lesson	Psalm	Second Lesson	Gospel
Revised Common	Num. 6:22-27	Psalm 8	Gal. 4:4-7 or Phil. 2:5-11	Luke 2:15-21
Episcopal (BCP)	Exod. 34:1-8	Psalm 8	Rom. 1:1-7	Luke 2:15-21
Roman Catholic	Num. 6:22-27	Ps. 67:2-3, 5-6, 8	Gal. 4:4-7	Luke 2:16-21
Lutheran (LBW)	Num. 6:22-27	Psalm 8	Rom. 1:1-7 or Phil. 2:9-13	Luke 2:21

FIRST LESSON: NUMBERS 6:22-27; EXODUS 34:1-8

Numbers 6:22-27. The ancient blessing of Aaron in Num. 6:22-26 is only loosely attached in the narrative to the prescriptions concerning nazirite vows in 6:1-21, but it stands at the end of a series of laws designed to maintain the holiness of the people who are called to follow a holy God (5:1—6:21). The benediction that assures the people of God's grace and peace rightly rests on the community that faithfully keeps itself in the proper state of purity in the presence of God. The sometimes tempting modern distinction between ritual and moral purity is really foreign to Numbers, as attested by the provisions for restitution in 5:5-10 that begin, "when a man or woman wrongs another, breaking faith with the LORD" (v. 6).

The words of the benediction may be among the oldest in the Hebrew Bible, since they are found on portions of sixth- or seventh-century B.C.E. silver amulets from Jerusalem, and they are reminiscent of other blessings in Scripture. Leviticus 9:22 pictures Aaron himself blessing the people after he has sacrificed a sin offering on their behalf, and pronouncing God's blessing on the people is one of the central functions of the priesthood. 2 Chronicles 30:27 describes the priestly blessing that follows Hezekiah's Passover celebration in terms that make explicit ancient Israel's understanding of blessing: "Then the priests and Levites stood up and blessed the people, and their voice was heard; their prayer came to [God's] holy dwelling in heaven." A blessing is thus an effectual prayer for divine benefit, what is sometimes called a performative utterance. The ancient Israelite priest who asks God's blessing on the people fully expects that what he says will happen. It is not mere wishful thinking or an expression of good will, as our casual "God bless you" follows a sneeze. A blessing is effectual because it comes from God, not from people.

The poetry of Num. 6:22-26 is ancient Hebrew parallelism. God's *blessing* confers the gifts of God's bounty—food, shelter, land, children, health—and God's *keeping* provides safety from harm. The shining light of God's *face* is the reflection of God's own glory, which is more the quality of God's presence than a specific attribute God possesses. God's intimate presence among the people brings grace, or the unmerited favor of one who enters into uncompelled covenant relationship with those who are loved simply because it is God's desire to love (cf. Pss. 67:1; 89:15). The lifting up of God's *countenance* borrows from the image of the royal court a moment when the monarch bestows particular largesse on a subject by raising his or her face, granting *shalom*. This peace is not only the absence of conflict, of course, but the active promotion of life in all its fullness.

Aaron's benediction is described in Num. 6:27 as putting God's name on the Israelites, a mark of possession, as a brand identifies the owner of an animal or—more metaphorically—as physical similarities among family members carry the mark of the family name. To wear God's name is also, however, to carry the promise of God's protection, as God's mark protected Cain, for example (Gen. 4:15). As the silver amulets engraved with the words of Num. 6:22-26 suggest, the wearing of God's name may have been literal as well as figurative for some ancient Israelites.

Exodus 34:1-8. After God initiates the covenant with Moses and the Israelites in Exod. 19:1—23:32, the people promise solemnly, "all the words that the LORD has spoken we will do" (24:3) and "all that the LORD has spoken we will do, and we will be obedient" (24:7). Moses then inscribes the covenant conditions (24:4), the people worship God (24:5-11), and God personally writes the commandments in stone (24:12), a phrase we commonly use to signify a permanent agreement. Moses then returns to the mountain, where God gives him elaborate and lengthy instructions for the preparation of the cult (25:1—31:17) that conclude with God's personally handing over the tablets of the law (31:18). The time Moses has spent with God, though, apparently makes the people impatient to be about the business of religion, and they urge Aaron to make alternative plans in Moses' absence (32:1), since conventional wisdom always says that a bird in the hand is worth two in the bush. Aaron consents to the plan, they forge a fertility god out of precious metals, and the people make their own cultic preparations that unwittingly (but ironically) mimic what God has commanded of Moses (32:2-6). God is understandably enraged by the fair-weather faithfulness of this so-called covenant people and vows to destroy them and save Moses (v. 10). But Moses pleads with God to spare the Israelites, on the basis of God's own reputation among the Egyptians (v. 12) and God's prior covenant with Abraham (v. 13), and begs God to "change your mind" (v. 12).

As God repented of having created at the time of the flood (Gen. 6:5) and was persuaded by Abraham to spare Sodom should just ten righteous souls be found there (Gen. 18:32), so in response to Moses "the LORD changed his mind about the disaster that he planned to bring on his people" (Exod. 32:14). For all his compassion in interceding for the idolatrous Israelites, Moses too is furious at them and repudiates their covenant with God by breaking the stone tablets at the foot of the mountain (32:19). God refuses at this point anymore to accompany the people in their wilderness trek (33:3) but yet again accedes to Moses' further plea on their behalf (33:14).

It is at this point, with the covenant made and the covenant broken, that this morning's lesson from Exodus 34 begins. "Cut two tablets of stone like the former ones," says God to Moses, "and I will write on the tablets the words that were on the former tablets, which you broke" (34:1). Covenant renewal, as the covenant itself, comes at God's initiative, even though it is Israel that has broken the first one. The instructions to Moses in vv. 2-4 deliberately recall the first set in Exodus 19, although oddly the commandments in 34:10-26 are not the same as those in Exodus 20, suggesting to many critics that this story once had an independent origin and was incorporated at a later date into the larger Exodus narrative. The focus in 24:1-8, however, is not on the provisions of the covenant itself but rather on its initiator.

At v. 5 God condescends to Moses and announces in a single word the divine name first revealed at the burning bush: "I AM" (Exod. 3:15). This is surely one of the most poignant and powerful dramatizations of divine forgiveness in all of Scripture. God starts all over with Moses, as if from the beginning. Not even the vision of the forgiving father who runs to meet his wayward son in Jesus' parable (Luke 15:11-32) or Hosea's frantic searching for Gomer carries this sense of deliberate decision to begin again the hard work of reconciliation that we see in Exodus 34. Theologians sometimes talk about a distinction between *de jure* and *de facto* forgiveness. Technical forgiveness, *de jure* forgiveness, is what a wife grants her adulterous husband with tears and through gritted teeth when he confesses and begs her not to divorce him. The proof of her words, though, comes later, after a hard time of renegotiating the marriage and more tears and more gritted teeth, when she forgives him *de facto* and one evening tosses him the dish towel and says, "OK, you can stay. I'll wash; you dry." In renewing the covenant God says to the Israelites, you can stay.

After pronouncing the divine name, God then elaborates on it with a summary of God's character. The Lord is above all abounding in *hesed*, which the NRSV translates "steadfast love" but is perhaps better understood as covenant loyalty (vv. 6-7). God's love for Israel survives even its appalling and ridiculous flirtation with Canaanite gods. God's mercy and grace endure even when the people are contemptuous of God. God forgives and forgives, and continues to hold the covenant bonds secure for thousands of generations, despite repeated transgression of God's law and offense against God's person (v. 7). But mercy and loyalty to the covenant do not by any means water down the demands of justice for those with whom God is in relationship. The consequences of sin reverberate "to the third and fourth generation" (v. 7), which is to say that we are as often punished by our sin as for it. Because God initiates covenant, God's character defines it, and that means human behavior must be measured by the justice as well as the mercy of God. The conventional opposition of justice to mercy is a human, not a divine, distinction, and is born of attempts to attain for oneself a measure of religious security rather than an awareness that God's holiness is loving and God's love is holy.

SECOND LESSON: ROMANS 1:1-7; PHILIPPIANS 2:1-13; GALATIANS 4:4-7

Romans 1:1-7. The salutation of the letter to the Romans identifies Paul in terms of his message. A previously unknown group of congregations in the capital city receives the *curriculum vitae* of a preacher who hopes to establish a mission base among them as he moves west to Spain (cf. 15:22-30). His gospel, he says, is about Jesus, whom he describes in two parallel clauses: physically Jesus is David's descendant (which recalls Nathan's oracle to the king in 2 Sam. 7:11-16), but he is designated God's descendant, God's son, by his resurrection from the dead. This adoptionist-sounding Christology (along the lines of Pss. 2:7 or 110:1, in which God "adopts" the king at his coronation) stands in some tension with Paul's customary language about Jesus. Elsewhere, he speaks as though Christ was preexistent with God (for instance, 2 Cor. 8:9, "though he was rich . . . he became poor," or Phil. 2:6-11, "though he was in the form of God . . . he took the form of a slave," and the ubiquitous phrase "God sent his Son"), and this makes most interpreters suspect Paul quotes here a portion of a confession of faith already known by the Christians in Rome. The effect of including this fragment of an early confession, even though it does not exactly express what the apostle usually says, is to establish a theological common ground with his readers who may have heard less-than-orthodox things about him from other sources (cf. 3:8). What sounds like a case of competing Christologies to those of us who stand on the other side of the fourth- and fifth-century christological controversies, though, would not likely have troubled Paul.

As Paul W. Meyer notes, "what is decisive for Paul about Jesus of Nazareth is God's identification with him" as Son of God in the resurrection, rather than any particular mechanics of that identification ("Romans" in *Harper's Bible Commentary* [ed. James L. Mays; San Francisco: Harper & Row, 1988], 1134).

As is customary in Hellenistic letters, Paul opens with his own name, but because his addressees have never met him (with the exception of the twenty-seven people he greets by name in 16:3-15!) he identifies himself first as a slave of Christ and second as one "called to be an apostle" (1:1). In the Greco-Roman world, a slave carries the stature and honor (or shame) of his or her master, so Paul's claim to be Christ's slave is not simply an expression of religious devotion. As Christ's slave Paul is one who approaches the house churches of Rome on behalf of Christ himself. As an apostle who has been called by God, Paul presents himself to the churches as one who speaks not on his own authority but on the authority of the one who has sent him. He will later tell the Roman believers that they too share his status as slave (6:17-18) and he will greet them as those who are also "called" by God (1:7), but his initial self-introduction is designed to gain himself a respectful hearing among strangers.

Paul says he has been "set apart for the gospel of God," a fitting reminder during this most christocentric season of the church year that it is the one God of Abraham, Isaac, and Jacob, the God who rescued Israel from Egypt and who raised Jesus from the dead, who joins our flesh in the babe of Bethlehem. God's good news, Paul says, has been God's intention for all time, because it is "promised beforehand . . . in the holy scriptures" (v. 2). Popular piety sometimes reduces the incarnation to something of a last-ditch effort, God's final resort after trying unsuccessfully through the law and the prophets to reach humankind. By contrast, in Rom. 1:2 Paul affirms God's consistency and faithfulness by saying that God has planned all along to send Christ. For all that the gospel announces a drastically new and ultimately transforming moment in God's redemption of creation (Paul uses the word "now" more frequently in Romans than in all the rest of his extant letters combined), it is at the same time profoundly consistent with God's previous ways with the world, as the rest of Romans (and particularly chapters 9–11) will explore. God is not predictable, but neither is God capricious. This radically new thing of the Christ-event is part and parcel of God's historic faithfulness.

The gospel Paul preaches concerns "Jesus Christ *our* Lord" (v. 4), yet another reminder to this unknown group of congregations that he writes to them as one of them. Through Christ, he says, "we have received grace and apostleship to bring about the obedience of faith" (v. 5), which might also

THE NAME OF JESUS (JANUARY 1)

be rendered "obedient faith" or "faithful obedience," that is, the obedience that results in faith. As Paul will argue at length later in the letter, God's law reaches its divinely ordained destination, achieves the goal for which it was intended, in the proclamation of God's impartial righteousness to all without regard for their religious heritage or moral probity (see especially 10:4). This means that the "obedience of faith" is scarcely the confusing clash of "law" with "gospel" or "works" with "faith" that some have heard it to be.

Paul preaches the gospel of God "among all the Gentiles for the sake of [God's] name" (1:5). At 2:24 he will quote Isa. 52:5 to say that "the name of God is blasphemed among the Gentiles" because of the covenant people's sin, but the notion is ubiquitous in the Hebrew Bible that God's name, God's reputation, God's character and honor are at stake in the just life and covenant faithfulness of God's people. What is at stake is not merely that human beings might say bad things about or ridicule God, but that God's sovereign integrity might be jeopardized when God's will is defied. When the psalmist says, for example, that the Lord "leads me in right paths for his name's sake" (23:3), he means that God guides him toward righteousness because that is what God does, that is the kind of God Yahweh is. For "all the Gentiles" not to come to obedient faith, Paul says, would put at risk the very character of God who is at once eternally faithful to Israel and impartially judges Jews and Gentiles alike. When he states the theme of his letter at 1:16, he will say the gospel is "the power of God for salvation *to everyone* who believes, *to the Jew first* and also to the Greek."

Verse 6 provides Paul's transition from his self-identification to the naming of his letter's recipients. They too are among those "called to belong to Jesus Christ" and so he greets them as "God's beloved . . . called to be saints" (v. 7). Just as Paul says of himself that he is called to be an apostle (v. 1) so the church is called to be saints. The word can also be translated "holy ones," since that is what saints are, people set apart by God, just as the apostle himself has been "set apart" for his work (v. 1). This grounding of an epistolary relationship, largely in the absence of a personal one, has strategic aims. Paul needs to establish sufficient rapport with the diverse Roman house churches (note the "all" at the beginning of v. 7) that they will together support his mission to Spain (15:24) and intercede with God on his behalf as he takes the collection from the Gentile churches to Jerusalem (15:30-31). Paul's aims are strategic, but should not be characterized as cynical or manipulative. The grace (*charis*) and peace he sends them in his greeting are not the "hello" of the conventional salutation in a letter written in Greek (*chairein*) or Hebrew (*shalom*), but are rather gifts from the God whose mission to the world Paul shares.

Philippians 2:1-13. The christological hymn Paul invokes in 2:6-11 stood alone before he quoted it, and it certainly might be preached again in isolation from its current literary context in Philippians, but it makes very little sense to truncate the poetry by beginning to read only at its second stanza, which is where the assigned lectionary passage begins. The inclusion of vv. 12-13 goes some distance toward acknowledging the paraenetic (or hortatory) function the hymn apparently serves in the letter, although Paul says more about what he thinks the Christ-hymn says about Christian life in 2:1-5 than he does in 2:12ff. To listen to the literary context makes the hymn less theologically or philosophically speculative and focuses it instead on the congregation's life. To hear it in the context where Paul quotes it draws from it a more incarnational point than to attend to the hymn alone. But church history is also replete with powerful sermons preached on speculative texts or from speculative stances. However a preacher decides to read the text in worship, interpretation ought at least to consider the hymn in its entirety. The following theological reflection on it takes the epistolary context seriously as well.

The first in a series of imperatives at the beginning of chapter 2 calls Paul's dear friends in Philippi to "make my joy complete" (2:2). Since he and they have united in a formal agreement called a *societas* or partnership (see above, the Second Sunday in Advent) to advance the gospel of Christ, and have therefore agreed to share together in the expense and labor as well as the benefits of their joint endeavor, Paul can call on their common understanding of what a *societas* demands of its partners. Paul will rejoice fully, that is, he will rejoice at the completion of the project, if the church is "*of the same mind,* having the same love, being in full accord and of *one mind*" (v. 2). This being "of the same mind" means they will all be pulling in the same direction for the success of the venture they have entered into together. This is not merely a predictable call for team spirit, however, as the following two sentences interpret what Paul means.

First, the Philippians are to put aside their personal ambitions. This in itself might be no more than a matter of a call for cooperation for the sake of a larger goal. But Paul goes a step further, to exhort believers to "regard others as better than [them]selves" (v. 3). This is not modesty that pretends one is not competent or that others are more able, but an active search for someone else's good at the expense of one's own. "Let each of you look not to your own interests," he says, "but to the interests of others" (v. 4). This rather than self-effacement is the true definition of "humility" (v. 3).

The "one mind" the church is to pursue is not simply a goal they have agreed on together, as would be true of a commercial *societas*, but is the very mind of Christ, which is why Paul says, "let the same mind be in you that was in Christ Jesus" (v. 5). Christ's mind in this regard is his intention, his direction, the purpose of his life that is described in the hymn that follows in vv. 6-11. That this particular mind rather than some other should form their partnership suggests that Paul's lauding of Jesus' preexistence and glorification by God by quoting the hymn function not so much to describe eternal christological verities or the calculus of redemption as to put flesh on the day-to-day life of believers in community. Whether the Philippians also know the hymn as Paul does is not clear, but the fact that he interrupts it at the end of the first stanza to insert a characteristic phrase of his own ("even death on a cross," v. 8) suggests that he may expect his hearers to recognize what he has done. If a contemporary preacher were to quote a familiar piece of poetry or a hymn with such an inserted phrase of interpretation would certainly draw the congregation's attention to the move.

The first half of the hymn proper (vv. 6-8) begins with a relative pronoun, "who," which strikes modern ears as odd, but was common in ancient hymns and creeds. It continues to describe Christ in two parallel but consecutive moments, the first when "he was in the form of God" (v. 6), the second when he "[took] the form of a slave" (v. 7). Paul is a Jew, at the center of his very being a monotheist, so it is not easy to see what he means by saying that a human being—even Christ—was "in the form of God." Does he mean that when Jesus had God's form he had God's "image" and "likeness," as Gen. 1:26 says all humanity does? The "form" of God also sounds like what the Bible says of God's "glory," the (only rarely) visible manifestation of God's being (Exod. 16:10; 24:16; Lev. 9:6, 23; Num. 14:10). If this is the reference in the hymn, it means that Jesus has divine status and reflects the character and being of God to a degree far greater than other human beings can or do. Perhaps the thought is of human beings before their corruption by sin, of Adam before the fall, or perhaps of Adam redeemed from the fall. In that case, then Jesus' obedience to God reverses and undoes the consequences of Adam's disobedience. Whether or not this is the thought of the original hymnwriter, it accords well with what Paul says in 2 Cor. 5:21, that God "made [Christ] to be sin who knew no sin."

This "equality with God" that Jesus exists in, his bearing God's form in a unique way, is not a possession he considers necessary to cling to. The "something to be exploited" (v. 6) of the NRSV translates a rare word whose roots lie in the verb "to seize." The image is of Jesus' not holding on for dear life to his rights as God's Son but of letting go of them in obedience to God. Jesus' emptying of himself (v. 7) uses the metaphor of a container that is prepared for a new function. He lets go of one "form" in order to take on another "form," that of a slave. Paul thinks of himself similarly in terms of a container at God's disposal when he says "we have this treasure [the gospel] in clay jars" (2 Cor. 4:7). "The form of a slave" is further defined in the hymn as being "in human likeness" and "in human form." Although the participle *genomenos* is frequently translated "being born," that is true only to the degree that a person "happens" or "becomes" at birth. The usual verbs associated with being born, *gennaō* and *tiktō*, are not used here as they are in the infancy narratives of Matthew or Luke. The hymn says that the one who shared God's form "happened" as a human being. This is a remarkable statement about divine humiliation, and may be the reason Paul chooses to quote the hymn at this point in his letter (note "humbled himself" in v. 8 and "in humility" in v. 3).

Jesus undergoes humiliation willingly rather than being compelled. His humbling of himself stands in parallel relation with and is therefore equivalent to his obeying God, and the emphasis falls on his willingness to do so rather than on God's demanding it. Obedience to the point of death is of course the ultimate obedience, but here Paul adds to the hymn's portrait of Jesus' fidelity to God's will the further humiliation of the *way* Jesus died. To the Galatians Paul quotes Deut. 21:23, "cursed is everyone who hangs on a tree" (Gal. 3:13) to show how Christ's becoming a curse for us frees us from the curse we bear ourselves. In the context of the Philippians hymn, Paul's reference to the cross as a particularly shameful, even cursed, form of execution emphasizes the depths to which Jesus obediently goes to accomplish God's saving intention.

The "therefore" of v. 9 initiates the second half of the hymn and traces the exaltation of the humiliated one. God "highly exalted him," meaning that God raised Jesus back to the status he originally shared with God, and "gave him the name that is above every name" (v. 9). God's exaltation of Jesus is his resurrection, since by raising him from the dead God endorses both Jesus and his death as the means of God's redemption. The name God bestows is not merely "Jesus"—a name, after all, that is carried by countless other men—but "Jesus Christ" (v. 11). The naming of the slave as the master (or lord) completes the reversal begun by the one who first exchanged God's form for that of human beings.

It is Jesus' obedience "to the point of death" and God's identification with that death that causes interpreters to think again of Adam in Genesis 2–3, even more than the possible allusion in the opening line of the hymn. The first human beings disobey God and eat the fruit that makes them "like God" (Gen. 3:5, 22) and they are therefore banned from the garden lest they "take also from the tree of life, and eat, and live forever" (3:22). Jesus, on the other hand, who already shares both God's form and God's life, obediently chooses human form and human death. Adam and Eve grasp at precisely what Jesus does not grasp (Phil. 2:6). Their punishment is mortality (Gen. 3:19); Jesus' reward is life from the dead (Phil. 2:9). Adam and Eve's disobedience brings a curse on the earth (Gen. 3:17); Jesus' exaltation evokes the praise of all things above, on, and below the earth (Phil. 2:10). Because Paul seems to argue from assumptions something like these in both Rom. 5:12-21 and 1 Cor. 15:20-23, it seems plausible that he understands the Christ-hymn in Philippians this way. If this is so, then his quoting of it to the Philippian Christians calls them to a radically cruciform life, embracing the redeemed and renewed human existence that is theirs through Christ's death and resurrection and themselves relinquishing their rights—and even their lives—for one another as Christ has for them.

(For Galatians 4:4-7, see the second lesson for the First Sunday after Christmas.)

GOSPEL: LUKE 2:21; 2:16-21; 2:15-21

(See the Gospel for The Nativity of Our Lord 1—Christmas Eve.)

Second Sunday after Christmas

Lectionary	First Lesson	Psalm	Second Lesson	Gospel
Revised Common	Jer. 31:7-14 or Sir. 24:1-12	Ps. 147:12-20 or Wis. 10:15-21	Eph. 1:3-14	John 1:(1-9), 10-18
Episcopal (BCP)	Jer. 31:7-14	Psalm 84 or 84:1-8	Eph. 1:3-6, 15-19a	Matt. 2:13-15, 19-23 or Luke 2:41-52 or Matt. 2:1-12
Roman Catholic	Sir. 24:1-4, 8-12	Ps. 147:12-15, 19-20	Eph. 1:3-6, 15-18	John 1:1-18 or 1:1-5, 9-14
Lutheran (LBW)	Isa. 61:10—62:3	Ps. 147:13-21	Eph. 1:3-6, 15-18	John 1:1-18

FIRST LESSON: ISAIAH 61:10—62:3; SIRACH 24:1-2, 8-12; JEREMIAH 31:7-14

Sirach 24:1-2, 8-12. The poetic praise of Dame Wisdom that is Sirach 24 recalls similar texts in Prov. 8:22—9:12; Job 28; and Bar. 3:9-37. Wisdom speaks in the first person as God's first creation or even God's helper in creation (24:3; cf. Prov. 8:22), sits on a throne in God's highest heaven (Sir. 24:4), and rules the entire earth as God's regent (v. 6). Wisdom then travels the earth seeking a home (v. 7) and God gives her specifically as a gift to Israel (v. 8); the wanderer finds a home among the covenant people whose own history has been marked by wandering.

This portrait of Wisdom as the peculiar possession of Israel moves an important step beyond the ancient Israelite wisdom thought that is much more universal and transnational in its outlook. This is the result of the development of wisdom thought toward the turn of the eras (Sirach comes from some time near the end of the second century B.C.E.). The ancient attitude that called people to observe the world and discern the truth of wisdom so as to become wise gives way to a much more self-consciously religious definition of wisdom. Under the pressure of postexilic life surrounded by varieties of pagan wisdom, Jews begin to narrow the range of access to God's wisdom, saying it resides in God's law. Sirach makes this explicit at several points, picturing Wisdom as incarnate in Torah. The final stanza of the poem praising Dame Wisdom summarizes the preceding: "All this is the book of the covenant of the Most High God, the law that Moses commanded us as an inheritance for the congregations of Jacob" (24:23).

(For Isaiah 61:10—62:3 and Jeremiah 31:7-14, see the first lesson for the First Sunday after Christmas.)

SECOND SUNDAY AFTER CHRISTMAS

SECOND LESSON: EPHESIANS 1:3-6, 15-18 (-19a)

Whereas Paul's letters generally begin with a salutation and move directly to a thanksgiving that telegraphs the basic concerns of the letter (Galatians is a notable exception in this regard), the writer of Ephesians inserts a long and rhetorically elegant benediction (1:3-14) between the two (1:1-2; 1:15-16). 2 Corinthians has something similar (1:3-4), as does 1 Pet. 1:3, so the move is not unprecedented, but the length and complexity of the blessing in Ephesians presents interpretive challenges. The lectionary reading adds to the challenge, combining as it does the first sentence of that blessing (vv. 3-6) with the thanksgiving proper (vv. 15-16) and the first sentence that states the theme of the letter (vv. 17-19). Ephesians is notable for its unusually long and complicated sentences with many dependent and relative clauses that are difficult to render into comprehensible English. Although v. 19 in fact concludes a sentence in Greek, not all English translations reflect that. The NRSV here makes a marked improvement over the RSV, since the end of v. 19 (although not its midpoint, as suggested by the lectionary) is indeed a plausible stopping place.

The blessing of God offers praise for what God has already accomplished on the church's behalf and sounds something like traditional Jewish blessings of God that function as a form of congratulation to those who hear them pronounced. 1 Peter 1:3-9 congratulates its recipients on their surviving by God's power (see 1:5) the social ostracism and cultural hostility they experience because of their profession of faith. Ephesians 1:3-14 congratulates believers for their receipt of the "spiritual blessings" (1:3) God has bestowed in Christ: adoption as God's children (v. 5), redemption that achieves forgiveness of trespasses (v. 7), wisdom and insight (v. 8), the inheritance of God's glory (v. 11), and the "seal" of the Holy Spirit (v. 14).

These blessings, the author says, are "in the heavenly places" (v. 3), a peculiar phrase that represents a single word used in a distinctive way by the writer of Ephesians. Other New Testament writers sometimes use the word "heavenly," but only as an adjective that modifies a specific noun, most often to distinguish that "heavenly" person or thing from something "earthly" (for instance, John 3:12; 1 Cor. 15:40). In Ephesians, though, what is "heavenly" is heaven itself, the places Christians reside with God. The risen Christ is seated at God's right hand "in the heavenly places" (Eph. 1:20; cf. Ps. 110:1) and Christians are similarly "seated" there with Christ (Eph. 2:6). There are rulers and authorities in the heavenly places to whom the church makes known God's wisdom in the gospel (3:10), but the heavenly places are also where the church's enemies, the "spiritual forces of evil," are to be found (6:12). The opening clause of the blessing in 1:3 pictures all the gifts God has given the church as being stored there "before the foundation of the world," kept in readiness until Christ arrives to distribute them (see Nils Alstrup Dahl, "Ephesians," in *Harper's Bible Commentary* [ed. James L. Mays; San Francisco: Harper & Row, 1988], 1212-219).

The first specific spiritual blessing, and the only one the lectionary passage puts in view, is God's adoption of believers as children (Eph. 1:5-6). This is the only place outside the undisputed Pauline letters where the word "adoption" is used, and is an example of Ephesians' familiarity with important Pauline ideas, even though those ideas do not always carry the same meaning as in Paul. The slogan quoted at Eph. 2:5 and interpreted in 2:8-9, for example, contains the familiar contrast between "grace" and "faith" on the one hand, and "works" on the other, but asserts that believers have already been "saved," something Paul consistently reserves for the eschatological future (cf. Rom. 5:9-10). So also with the notion of adoption does the writer of Ephesians appropriate Paul's language and basic thought and adapt it by interpretation to a new situation. Paul says that Israel is adopted by God (Rom. 9:4) and that Christians receive the "spirit of adoption" at baptism, when they are given the right to call God *Abba* (8:15; cf. Gal. 4:6). But for Paul, there is nevertheless a measure of our status as God's children that remains to be completed at Jesus' parousia, since we also "wait for adoption, the redemption of our bodies" (Rom. 8:23) just as the creation awaits "the revealing of the children of God" (8:19). In Ephesians, however, there is no such eschatological reservation, as Ernst Käsemann calls it, for Christians have already been given *every* spiritual blessing and they already sit with Christ as adopted children in God's presence in the heavenly places (1:3).

What prompts this focus on the current security of the church, this concern to assure the letter's readers that they are safely children in God's family without any thought that their redemption is still to come? The author apparently senses that the congregation to which he writes is in great danger, both from within and without. The call to unity in 4:1-16 with its lengthy description of Christ's varying gifts sounds like a response to competition for leadership in the church, and the reference to people's being "blown about by every wind of doctrine" in 4:14 suggests that the struggle may include a doctrinal dispute as well (cf. "Let no one deceive you," 5:6). So also, the church's ethnic composition may be a factor that threatens its security. The community seems to be heavily Gentile in background and there are therefore likely few Jews (2:11-22; 4:22-24). It may be that the Gentile majority scorns the Jewish minority or that the few remaining Jews are contemptuous of the Gentiles whose welcome into the church in large numbers appears to threaten their identity as God's covenant people.

SECOND SUNDAY AFTER CHRISTMAS

Whichever is the case (and we know of both sorts of situations in the early church), the author repeatedly asserts the unity and interdependence of Jew and Gentile in the church, what he calls "the mystery of God's will" (1:9; cf. 3:1-13; 6:19).

The author also warns against external threats to the church's life: "Be careful then how you live . . . because the days are evil" (5:15-16), he says, and "our struggle is not against enemies of blood and flesh, but against . . . evil in the heavenly places" (6:10-17). The nature of that evil and the identities of its earthly agents remain obscure, but because the earliest mentions of the letter by Christian readers and its traditional connection to Ephesus all associate it with the province of Asia Minor, it is possible that the same cultural hostility experienced by some other early Christians also prompts the writing of Ephesians. All the New Testament literature that is connected with Asia Minor reflects a situation of conflict between Christians and their non-Christian neighbors. Patmos, the island of John's exile (Rev. 1:9) is just off the coast of Ephesus, which was known to be a stronghold of enthusiastic paganism at the end of the first century. Acts 19:23-41 records an angry pagan crowd's resistance to Christian preaching with the cheer "great is Artemis of the Ephesians!" (vv. 28, 34). Paul writes in 1 Cor. 15:32 that he "fought with beasts [that is, magicians] in Ephesus." 1 Peter counsels believers to maintain exemplary moral behavior in public because it is certain they will be maligned by outsiders simply because they are Christians (2:12; 3:16; 4:4, 14), and Col. 4:5-6 similarly urges its readers to preserve irenic relations with non-Christians. The same attitude is shared by 1 and 2 Timothy and Titus, documents also thought to have originated in Ephesus toward the end of the first century. In response to a sense of imminent peril from these multiple sources, then, the author of Ephesians invokes the authority and tradition of Paul's preaching to strengthen the internal stability of the congregation against divisive struggles for leadership and ethnic disputes and to shore up its defenses against attack from outsiders.

The author prays thankfully for the church's life and faith (1:15-16) and asks God for wisdom on their behalf (v. 17). The purpose of that wisdom, which is the capacity to discern God or to understand "revelation," is that the believers will be able to know three things: the "hope" to which God has called them (v. 18), the "riches" they will inherit from God (v. 18), and the great "power" of God that is at work among them. The three are functionally synonymous in Ephesians, all describing the destiny Christians share with Christ as they live forever in God's presence "in the heavenly places" (1:20).

GOSPEL: JOHN 1:1-18; MATTHEW 2:13-15, 19-23; LUKE 2:41-52

Matthew 2:13-23. Just as in a dream an angel announces Jesus' birth to Joseph in Matt. 1:20 and in another dream an angel warns the wise men in 2:12 and Joseph in 2:13 of Herod's threat to the young child Jesus, so now an angel again appears in a dream to direct Joseph how he is to care for his new family. The function of these dreams in the beginning of Matthew seems to be to assure the reader that God is in control of a story that might otherwise appear chaotic, with characters moving here and there at will. The lectionary passage leaves out the story of Herod's slaughter of the innocents in vv. 16-18, but that part is as essential to Matthew's story as the story of Joseph's flight to and return from Egypt.

The story of chapter 2 to this point is suffused with what Krister Stendahl called the questions "from whom and from where?" ("Quis et Unde? An Analysis of Matthew 1–2," in *Judentum, Urchristentum: Kirche* [ed. W. Eltester; Berlin: Topelmann, 1960], 94–105). In the first half of his birth and infancy narrative, Matthew details Jesus' ancestry and describes the circumstances of his birth (Matthew 1). In the second half, which comprises chapter 2, place names appear in each episode of the narrative. Jesus is born in "Bethlehem of Judea" (2:1), whose biblical identity is discussed in Mic. 5:2 (Matt. 2:5-6) and where Herod murders all the children under two years of age (2:16-18), the wise men are "from the East" (2:1) and return after paying homage to Jesus "to their own country" (2:12), Herod "and all Jerusalem" worry about the magi's report about a newborn king (2:3), and finally Joseph is sent by God to take "the child and his mother" from Bethlehem to Egypt (2:13) and from Egypt to Nazareth (2:23). Furthermore, the three most significant geographical locations in Matthew's story—Bethlehem, Egypt, and Nazareth—are described with Bible verses. Bethlehem is destined to be the birthplace of the Davidic king by words from Micah 2 (Matt. 2:6), Egypt is the place from which God calls "my son" according to Hos. 11:1 (Matt. 2:15), Herod's murder of the children is a fulfillment of Jer. 31:15 (Matt. 2:18), and (although the words cannot in fact be found in the Bible) Matthew thinks Jesus will live and grow up in Nazareth because of a prophecy he cites at 2:23, "He shall be called a Nazorean."

This remarkable attention to geography in chapter 2 suggests that the evangelist is as concerned to identify the origin of his main character in terms of *place* as much as the genealogy and annunciation he uses in chapter 1 show Jesus' origin in terms of *persons*. This dual focus on Jesus' origins allows Matthew to set the agenda for the rest of his Gospel. The genealogy identifies him as "the son of David, the son of Abraham" (1:1), although by adoption, since it is Joseph's ancestors who are listed. The

SECOND SUNDAY AFTER CHRISTMAS

angelic annunciation to Joseph of Mary's virgin pregnancy identifies Jesus as "God with us" (1:23) in much the same way Luke has Gabriel tell Mary more explicitly that her child will be "the Son of the Most High" (Luke 1:32). The narrative in Matthew 2, by means of its emphasis on place names, says that Jesus is not only a Davidic king descended from Abraham and related to God in a supernatural way, he is also the new Moses who interprets God's law in an equally supernatural way.

From nearly the moment he is born, the child Jesus is threatened by an evil ruler who learns about him through the medium of dreams granted to wise men. This calls to mind to anyone steeped in the Bible as Matthew clearly is the story of the Israelites' sojourn to Egypt, facilitated by Joseph's dream interpretations, and their ultimate imprisonment there ("Now a new king arose over Egypt, who did not know Joseph," Exod. 1:8). Herod's response to the news of Jesus' birth and the heavenly portents accompanying it is to trick the wise men into finding the baby for him (2:7-8), ostensibly to worship him (v. 8) but really to eliminate the competition (vv. 16-18). Herod's slaying of all the children easily evokes memories of Moses. Both the story in Exodus 1–2 of Pharaoh's attempt to limit the number of Israelites by enlisting the Hebrew midwives to murder male babies and the later story in Exod. 12:29-32 of the plague of the deaths of firstborn children come to mind when Matthew says Herod "sent and killed all the children who were two years old or under" (Matt. 2:16-18). Just as the baby Moses is miraculously saved from the Pharaoh's plot by the cleverness of his mother and sister, only to grow up in Pharaoh's own house (Exod. 2:1-10), so the baby Jesus is miraculously rescued from harm by his father's righteous attentiveness to divine guidance (2:13-16; cf. 1:19). In an ironic twist, Matthew has Joseph take Jesus and Mary *to* Egypt where there is safety from Herod's rage, reversing the direction of Moses' flight with the people of Israel *from* the dangers of Egypt. Finally, just as God directs Moses to lead the people of Israel to the land God has promised, so God directs Jesus' father to bring him to the very town—Nazareth—which God has destined to be his home for most of his life.

This description of Jesus in terms deliberately designed to make the reader think of Moses serves a larger purpose in Matthew's Gospel than simply to make his birth and childhood special. When Jesus describes authentic life in God's kingdom in his so-called Sermon on the Mount (chapters 5–7), the reader cannot help but think of Moses on Mount Sinai. Jesus' remarkable freedom with respect to Scripture derives from his status as God's Son who is greater than the temple (12:6), as David's Son who is greater than Solomon (12:42), and as the Messiah who has Moses' own authority to interpret God's law (cf. "you have heard that it was said to those of ancient times. . . . But I say to you . . ." [5:21, 27, 31, 33, 38, 43]).

Great gallons of ink and reams of paper have been expended by interpreters to figure out what Matthew thinks it means for Jesus to be "called a Nazorean" (2:23), and little consensus exists. The sentence itself or some variation on it cannot be satisfactorily located in Scripture, which may explain why this one alone of his "formula quotations" Matthew says was spoken "through the prophet*s*," and there is little evidence to suggest where he may have heard or read it. Since the word *nazaraios* in Matt. 2:23 is a plausible reading of the Greek translation of the word "nazirite," used in Judges 13:5, 7 to describe Samuel as one "set apart" or "consecrated," Matthew may have that story in mind. Alternatively, he may be thinking of another Hebrew word, *nezer*, which means "branch," a technical term for the Messiah that has a similar sound and is found in numerous prophetic texts. Whatever its source, the "Nazorean" label is essential to Matthew's description of Jesus because it locates him in the village everyone knows him to have lived in: Nazareth. As John P. Meier observes, though, because Matthew thinks Jesus' hometown is Bethlehem, Nazareth in the region of the Galilee functions more as a place of exile than of home for Jesus until the end of the story when he returns to his rightful home in Judea, to Jerusalem, to be crucified (*Matthew* [NTM 3; Wilmington, Del.: Michael Glazier, 1980], 16).

Even non-Christians in the first century know that Jesus is from Nazareth, an otherwise utterly unremarkable widening of the road in the Galilee. The village is named nowhere in ancient literature outside the New Testament and elicits wisecracks from the likes of Nathanael in John 1:46, "Can anything good come out of Nazareth?" Everyone knows Jesus comes from Nazareth, but Jews and Christians also know that the Bible says the Davidic Messiah will come from David's hometown Bethlehem (Mic. 5:2). The Fourth Evangelist solves the problem by asserting that Jesus' physical origin is irrelevant. It does not matter whether Jesus comes from Bethlehem or Nazareth because Jesus really comes from God (John 7:42; cf. 7:27-28). Luke solves the problem another way, by inventing the peculiar story of the census that forces Mary and Joseph to travel to Bethlehem where—providentially—Mary has her baby. Matthew, however, believes that Jesus is in fact a native of David's city because he is in fact David's descendant. His challenge, then, is the opposite of Luke's, for he must find a way to move the family from Bethlehem to the place that he knows Jesus' life was largely spent and from which his ministry began.

This creative movement of the story's characters across the map in Matthew 2 is no mere biblicism, as if all Matthew cared about were Jesus' ability to fit the terms of prophecy and thus be "proved" to be the Messiah. Matthew does not read the Bible to discover whether or not Jesus is the Messiah. Because he already knows that Jesus is the Messiah Matthew reads the Bible through that interpretive lens. Consequently, Micah's prophecy about Bethlehem and the story of Moses, that definitive narrative of Israel's identity, are both transformed under the influence of Matthew's Christian faith in Jesus of Nazareth, crucified and raised.

(For John 1:1-18, see the Gospel for The Nativity of Our Lord 2— Christmas Day; for Luke 2:41-52, see the Gospel for the First Sunday after Christmas.)